The Plume Anthology of Poetry 2013

edited by Daniel Lawless

MadHat Press
Asheville, North Carolina

MadHat Press
MadHat Incorporated
PO Box 8364, Asheville, NC 28814

The material in this anthology is selected from
PlumePoetry.com
by Editor Daniel Lawless
with the assistance of Production Managers
Jonathan Penton & Alex Cigale

ISBN 978-1-941196-02-1 (paperback)

Cover art by Laurie Simmons
Book and cover design by MadHat Press

www.PlumePoetry.com
www.MadHat-Press.com

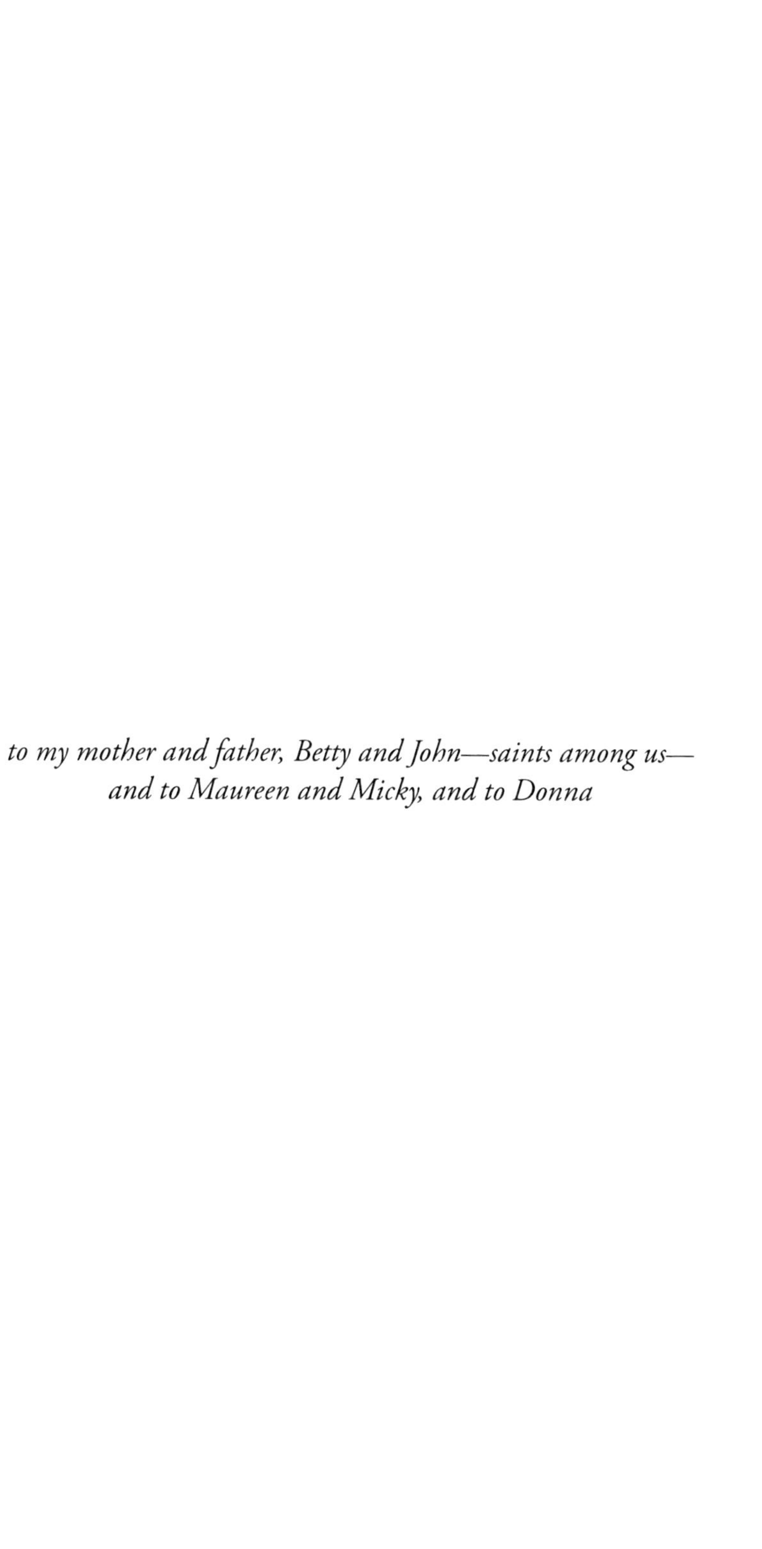

*to my mother and father, Betty and John—saints among us—
and to Maureen and Micky, and to Donna*

"*Plume* continues to publish amazing poets in beautiful formats—both online and in-print. The magazine has an exciting vision, embracing a broad gamut of poetries, including collaborations. The work has a consistently intriguing quality about the joys and unsettling aspects of being alive."
~ Denise Duhamel

"I've never seen a literary magazine become so important so quickly. I have no idea how Daniel Lawless does it, but I dare anyone to find another journal that contains 1) the high quality of the individual poems, 2) the wide range of voices and styles, and 3) the large number of leading voices in contemporary American poetry. I would love to see all these poets in the same room, but I'll take them here, all in the same book."
~ Jim Daniels

"*Plume*'s apparent lack of a narrow editorial policy (except a fondness for interesting poems) makes for lots of strange bedfellows, but what was the last time that was a bad idea?"
~ Billy Collins

"The list of contributors to this second *Plume* anthology is testimony to editor Danny Lawless's open secret: He's highly selective and thrillingly inclusive. His brilliance lies in assembling a community of poets and celebrating the glorious literary freedom of their work. *Plume* keeps giving us back what we always wanted from poetry—the voice of the human heart speaking to us with passion, intelligence, wit, ferocity, and imaginative aplomb.
~ David Huddle

"*Plume* is one of the most exciting, eclectic gatherings of writers on the web. Editor Daniel Lawless has a knack for putting together voices that create surprising neighborhoods of words, related in complex ways that only gradually reveal themselves. It's one of very few webzines that I always read."
~ Chase Twichell

"*Plume* is rapidly becoming one of the best places in America to read poetry, on-line and in print, thanks to the untiring efforts of Danny Lawless. It's where to find dazzling work by new and established writers, and, thanks to the new technology, it is available instantly to readers by the millions. *Plume* proves once more that poetry is essential to our lives, and that 'Men die every day for want of what is found in it.'"
~ Grace Schulman

"*Plume* magazine, and now the second volume of its *Plume Anthology of Poetry*, is a beautifully edited and stylishly presented cross-section of what is alive and well in contemporary poetry. I always feel honored and a part of a distinguished family when Daniel Lawless selects one of my poems."
~ Diane Wakoski

"I usually hate to read poems on the computer but Plume has changed my mind. It is attractive, well-edited, and possesses the compelling virtue of being concise—not too many poems, not too few. Since I always end up wanting to print out one or two, I'm grateful for Danny Lawless's equally exciting, good-looking, and well-chosen, *Plume* anthologies."
~ Lawrence Raab

"*Plume* is a gem—in the rare-and-wondrous-find sense. Each issue is a hand-plucked, precisely curated composition, tended with great care, full of mystery, and delivering batches of the freshest, most provocative, and necessary writing around. Danny Lawless's vision is exquisite."
~ Lia Purpura

"Blurbing a book you're in is like telling people where to find the baby in the King cake. It's not fair, but if the cake is good, the baby's lagniappe. The main thing is the cake."
~ Andrei Codrescu

"*Plume* is a new force in the poetry world, bringing together, in its online zine and in this anthology, a unique, eclectic and impressive group of poets."
- Rae Armantrout

"Of all the things that might claim one's attention, and they are in the multitudes! *Plume* is well worth making time for since it isn't just another magazine. Its difference? Wonderful work, on the edge, room for play and dash, new forms, a great discerning editor in Danny Lawless!"
- Tess Gallagher

"It's a fantastic poetry magazine. A selection of work from American and International poets, emerging and established."
- Anzhelina Polonskaya

"Like all the poets who appear in the *Plume Anthology of Poetry 2013*, I'm delighted to be included in this dazzling collection of U.S. and International poetry. The range of poems is stunning in its breadth, depth, and variety; running from Catullus to Jorie Graham, from New Orleans to Taipei. Editor Daniel Lawless has an unerring eye for selecting and publishing complex poetry filled with aesthetic surprises."
- Mary Mackey

"*Plume* is a gathering place where strangers become old friends. Each issue is a celebration of images and words that touch the heart and bind us together as community."
- Lawrence Matsuda

"*Plume*, the most exciting online magazine of the decade, has consistently surprised and delighted readers, attracting the best contemporary writers of the day. With every issue I am reminded of the early Muslim tale that Allah's first invention was the pen, or as the French might say, *un stylo a plume*. With offerings from acclaimed American writers as diverse as Denise Duhamel, Lydia Davis, Sharon

Olds and Billy Collins as well as from International heavy-hitters Yves Bonnefoy, Cees Nooteboom, and Karl Krolow, the second anthology of *Plume* is nothing short of a must-read."
- Nin Andrews

"The first word I remember using to describe Danny Lawless's online *Plume* was the word elegant. And now I discover that the word derives from a Latin verb for *to select*. *Plume* endeavors to select and showcase—yes, elegantly—the best poems of the twenty-first century. *Plume* not only encourages, it honors poetry."
- Ron Smith

"Though I've been known to shy away from on-line publications, I'm an avid reader of *Plume*, a beautifully designed monthly periodical featuring an international selection of works by some of today's best poets. Hard to beat that."
- William Trowbridge

"*Plume* (Noun): An anthology or journal of fine writing edited with passion and immaculate attention to detail.
"Plume (Verb): To erupt with energy, enthusiasm and poetic spirit. To dazzle.
"Derivative of Plume: Plumelike (Adjective): As fine as down and as lively as peacock feathers.
"Origins of *Plume*: American, but with an internationalist bent, some time during the 2000s."
- John Kinsella

"*Plume* magazine is an anomaly of taste: any literary dwelling that can shelter under one roof a family of poets as distantly related as Rae Armantrout, James Richardson, Kim Addonizio, Jorie Graham, Linda Pastan, G.C. Waldrep, Grace Schulman, Carl Phillips, Sharon Olds, Billy Collins, and more, must be both capacious and *odd*. What in the world unites these writers, one thinks? And then one reads an issue of *Plume* with the dawning recognition what they have in common

is Danny Lawless, the founder and editor of this superb new journal. Lawless has the audacity to choose the poets he loves, and believes are writing *good* poetry, no matter on what wildly disparate branch of the family tree he finds them. And then he gets these poets to send him poems. *Plume* establishes its place on the literary scene somewhere above fashion, apart from all questions of Hipster vs. . . . Whatever. The work within its pages has the unpredictable, idiosyncratic strength of things that haunt, and may endure."
- Jeffrey Skinner

"Always astonishing and diverse in content, *Plume* is one of our most elite and essential online journals and a roving museum of contemporary poetry curated by Daniel Lawless. 'Glancing blow' after glancing blow, it makes me hungry, ad infinitum, for the strange and beautiful—and the annual anthology is a sumptuous feast of enduring American poetry."
- Mark Irwin

"Like a bird landing in the absent shadow of a bird,
Plume has gorgeously and unabashedly
taken up residence inside an inner vane, an ache
in contemporary poetry, and sunk its hooklets in.
Now many of us cannot exist without it,
so drab and songless does a world without *Plume* seem to seem...."
- Robin Behn

"In less than three years, Daniel Lawless has created, in the online journal *Plume*, an exciting outlet for contemporary poetry, including translations. In this second annual *Plume Anthology*, he continues his practice of gathering a wide-ranging group of aesthetically diverse poets, almost all of them represented by previously unpublished poems."
- Martha Collins

"Like *Antaeus* and *Ironwood*, two of the greatest American poetry magazines of the past fifty years, *Plume* is eclectic in the most

purposeful and pleasurable of ways. In a very short amount of time, Danny Lawless has made it a 'must-read' like no other. *Plume* is one of my favorite sources for new poetry—online or in print. Thoughtful, entertaining, capacious, with no use for aesthetic axe-grinding, its highly-enriched oxygen will add energy to your life!"
- David Rivard

Preface
Linda Pastan

I have come late to the Internet—I almost gave away the computer my children insisted on buying me. But like new converts to anything, I am now an enthusiast, the one in the family who checks her e-mail almost hourly. And when I finish my email, it has become a pleasure to turn to a poem or two online, particularly a poem as carefully chosen and presented as the poems in *Plume* are. What better way to start the morning?

Still, I will always prefer the feel of a real book or journal in my hand, the heft of it, the subtle odor of paper. With the arrival of this new *Plume* anthology, I can have my cake and eat it. *Plume* has dedicated itself to publishing online the best new poems it can find, and now they have produced an anthology I can hold in my hand—a real book.

Speaking of cake, it seems to me that anthologies are a bit like menus—you can read the poems in one or two long sittings, following the editor's arrangement (in this case alphabetical) as with a tasting menu; or you can snack on them from time to time—ordering a poem here, a poem there—whenever you are hungry. And there are many treats to sustain you in this volume: a fine mix of established poets and new ones, of the lyric and the narrative, the playful and the meditative, and often the dark.

I started at the beginning with Dick Allen's poem about ants and will not look upon an ant the same way again. There are other animal poems to ponder, among them Carl Dennis's "Animal Husbandry," Martha Serpas's cattle egrets, John Kinsella's lambs. And poems about the visual arts—another favorite subject of mine—two of them by Lawrence Raab and David Huddle. There are poems about politics (in the largest sense), poems about landscape, poems about poems.

It is a pleasure to find so many poets here whose work I have savored for years: Sharon Olds, David Wagoner, Billy Collins, Roseanna

Warren, to name just a few. And of course one of the purposes of a good anthology, or a good journal for that matter, is to introduce us to poets we don't yet know so we can keep an eye on them, look for their work in other magazines, seek out their books. I was surprised at how many of the poets included here were new to me, good strong voices that I had somehow overlooked. Now I can look forward to finding more of their work, in future issues of *Plume*, of course, as well as elsewhere.

A plume can be a puff of smoke—a signal in the ether of cyberspace—or it can be an old-fashioned quill pen made from the feather of a real bird. What a fitting title, then, for a magazine which, with the publication of this anthology, so thoughtfully offers both.

Introduction

Daniel Lawless

Recently, one of our new contributors e-mailed me, noting his pleasure in having one of his poems accepted for publication in an online issue of *Plume*. Not unusual—the poets we publish have been uniformly generous and courteous in equal measure—but I recall also the remark he made at the conclusion of his short message: "Thanks for letting me join the club."

I think of this now, as I write, and what that word "club" connotes. *Not*, I hope, or at least not primarily, *exclusion* in any of its more well-known and often nefarious forms (velvet ropes, privileged mustachioed gentlemen of another era, etc.), which come to mind all too readily. But something more like the unassuming province of the hobbyist or schoolchild: a *gathering*, instead, familial, intimate, open to all of like mind and requiring no sponsor, no guide or fees, unattuned to gender, creed, financial status (needless to say, poets!) No, merely the love of poetry to bind us relative few—let's face it—together. The only password: beauty.

Still, I am not altogether a naïf. If there is to be a club, exclusion necessarily rears its head, yes? For even in such a venture as our own, so small, so unassuming, there must be those who are "in" and those who are "out"—our grateful contributor's remark wouldn't make sense if this were not the case. And so I grant you, reader of this short introduction, this—and yet: how I struggle against it, how it chafes. Because though *Plume* is open to all who love poetry, not all who love poetry (and it is the rare lover of poetry who does not also write it) can be represented in our pages. Nor should they be, as anyone who has glanced at the Submissions page of any journal of the arts, or found herself at an open-mic night at her local tavern. (Here it should be noted that the present anthology comprises, by rough estimate, 90% new work, previously unpublished in *Plume* or anywhere else.)

So, what is an editor to do but define the terms of that exclusion as narrowly as possible? And *that*, I believe—again, hope—is what we *have* done, over some two and a half years now. It is, as many have remarked, our signature achievement, such as it is: eclecticism, heterogeneity, whatever you wish to name it. Evidence for which can be produced with the perusal of a single issue—say, December's, 2013, to choose at random a recent sample. Here among others we find the following: Linda Pastan, at the peak of her powers in her eighth decade; a graphic comic from Bianca Stone, a poet and artist a third her age, perhaps; the rigorous historical work of Brian Culhane; surrealist-inflected prose poems from David Shumate; the Ecuadorean poet Ana Minga, whose work has been published to date mostly in small presses; Sophie Cabot Black, whom most readers know from her frequent contributions to the *New Yorker* and the *Atlantic*; the celebrated—and darkly hilarious—Tony Hoagland; Angie Estes, a finalist for the Pulitzer; Vadim Mesyats, a poet whose novel was shortlisted for the Russian Booker Prize; Vénus Khoury-Ghata, who collaborated on *Europe* magazine, directed by Louis Aragon, and a winner of the Prix Goncourt for Poetry, translated by the great Marilyn Hacker; Andrea Cohen, Amy Beeder, and Rachel Zucker—as different form one another as from their predecessors in this review.

And to draw these diverse talents together, for what purpose? Surely not for eclecticism's sake alone, or god forbid, to *educate*, to *expose to new things*: I do not think, as I make up each issue, "ah, we need a bit of X, then a pinch of y, *there*, that's the ticket." (Although it may seem so.) Rather, I cull each issue—and this anthology you hold in your hands—from our backlist of poems, selecting those that it seems to me will play with one another to mutual benefit, will scrap sometimes, and vex, elevate and echo, and, yes, mutter their hellos and speedily part ways, surprised and aghast to have found themselves at a party to which *he* or *she* was invited.

And last, make no mistake, it is I who make these decisions. My tastes and predilections, my curious long-held affinities and inexplicable antipathies, that create these silent hootenannies. For that I alone take responsibility: I, the curator of innumerable failures and occasional successes as well as well-intentioned *longeurs* and sudden pratfalls. For that, and to those whose work I have passed on (only to see it rise heroically in other pages) or delayed printing beyond all decency, I apologize. I wish I could do this better, but I probably can't.

Daniel Lawless
Editor, Plume
8 December 2013

CONTENTS

Creased Map of the Underworld

~ Kim Addonizio

Nothing is so beautiful as death,
thinks Death: stilled lark on the lawn,
its twiggy legs drawn up, squashed blossoms
of skunks and opossums on the freeway,
dog that drags itself trembling down
the front porch step, and stops
in a black-gummed grimace
before toppling into the poppies.
The ugly poppies. In Afghanistan
they are again made beautiful
by a mysterious blight. Ugly
are the arriving American soldiers, newly shorn
and checking their email,
but beautiful when face-up in the road
or their parts scattered
like bullet- or sprinkler-spray
or stellar remains. Lovely
is the nearly expired star
casting its mass into outer space,
lovelier the supernova
tearing itself apart
or collapsing like Lana Turner
in Frank O'Hara's poem.
Nothing is so beautiful as a poem
except maybe a nightingale,
thinks the poet writing about death,
sinking Lethe-wards. Lovely river
in which the names are carefully entered.
In this quadrant are the rivers of grief and fire.
Grid north. Black azimuth.
Down rivers of *Fuck you*s and orchids

steer lit hearts in little boats
gamely making their way,
spinning and flaming, flaming
and spiraling, always down—
down, the most beautiful of the directions.

Studio in Gotland

~ Meena Alexander

For Cecilia Edefalk

I was on an island where few birds call.
Old trees swirled in the wind

The door to my studio tore off,
Stones struck clouds, church bells echoed

– Earthly unsettlement.
Forced to go on, what did I do?

I pulled down a wall,
Set up another with pasteboard,

Tacked a strip of mirror all along the floor
Till white plaster was afloat, gravity unhinged.

The lights I had set up fell to one side
I stepped through the mirror to touch her –

She was that sort of being, what was the word
You gave me – *sakshi*, yes that.

No one would see her seeing I thought
Without themselves being altered in some way

So in the end she could have a chance
Of being saved from all the body remembers.

I took the face, making it very precise,
Filling in the eyes with several strokes

Reddening under the lids – fire turned to blood,
Each element as the Gnostics tell us

Resolved into its own roots.
The neck of course is simple and straight.

She is in a white dress as usual,
A child whose mother

Takes pleasure in dressing her well.
In the end my hands were pocked

And bruised with paint
And when I lifted them off the canvas

I felt something warm,
Very like torn skin fluttering off.

How to Avoid Being Nibbled to Death by Ants

~ Dick Allen

When they approach you in a straight line,
as in an ellipses. . . . . ,
you can veer to the left or right while saying to yourself,
"My toes are my own. You shall not have my toes,"
or hum "Ain't Misbehavin'" or "The Theme from *Picnic*."

If you have to stay in one place for a long time,
surround yourself with candied orange peels
and never call upon your past to save you. Your past
is a thick envelope of excuses
you should have left behind in some office storage bin.

Although ants are tiny misshapen hourglasses on their sides,
and resemble people seen from on top of the Empire State Building,
one ant by itself is hardly there, forlorn as a tiny pencil mark
not quite erased. Still, in their aggregate,
ants can bring you down to the level of shady footprints.

Sweet excesses attract them: excessive arrogance,
excessive humility. So don't rub your hands together
while you gloat. If you absolutely must gloat,
do it by yourself in a dusky basement. As for being humble,
nothing attracts an ant so much as when you identify with it.

Don't crumble your bread! Although your back itches,
don't roll in the dirt. If you have a choice,
choose what Buddha called "the middle way." And always pay attention
to the kind of corners where spiders surreptitiously
may lay their eggs. You will likewise find ants there.

Mainly, should they start to feast on you
despite your precautions and any other warnings,
you can always resort to jumping into a river
and hang on for dear life to a bridge abutment
or a steady rock as you watch them float away.

Victorian Dreaming

~ Nathalie Anderson

I figure it thus: a man stands all night
at a stand-up desk, stands figuring. Sums
scratched to foolscap scraps, snatched up, scattered – he
scarcely notices, his fair-hand crab-crawling
the brass-bound ledger, cross-copying out
meticulous accounts – best copperplate,
best boilerplate, each seven and zed crossed twice
for elegance, each g and y descending
into flourishings. Cuts quite the figure: sleeves
banded back and the cuffs scuffed to fraying,
wrists scrubbing the desk's edge till both patina,
cheek smudged where for a moment he propped it
dotting subtly the splattered blotter,
and the back straining tall, the weight shifted
hip to hip, the thighs clenched, the calves cramping,
even the arches braced against their fall,
eyes opened so long in ghastly gaslight
he thinks he sees beneath his feet the carpet writhe.

And writhe it does, what with the moths mating –
that twitch, that wing-throb – and the eggs hatching out –
that shuddering lather – and the maggots
urgent, pale pulsing slugs, each swallowing
its thread, gnawing it down to its nub; knots
unknotted – figure that! – strand by strand through
the deep-dyed wool; the bold geometries
and arabesques turned tatty, threadbare; and
all knitted, knotted back in tight cocoons, tinged
each with hints of former hues, the rose blanched,
the gold gone sallow, blue ashen, lilac
a dusky shadow. So at night's end, when

they open to the flit and tizzy of
new-hued moths, it's a knot garden rising,
a haze exotic in the air, before
he turns to look, and it all unravels.

Therapies

~ Nin Andrews

after Julio Cortazar

A man receives a counseling degree and opens a practice at a prestigious clinic on Chagrin Boulevard in Cleveland, Ohio. No sooner does he open his door then a patient arrives, flings his body on thehis couch and begins to complain that he is always cold. Not only is he always cold, but he never has sex. Not only does he have never have sex, but he lacks desire. He is like a crust of bread tossed to the birds, that even the birds won't peck at. *Do you know what that's like?* he asks, tears flowing fast. He reaches into his pocket and pulls out a handkerchief and a crumpled poem. *Only poetry can explain my misery now*, he says, as he reads aloud in a trembling voice:

My body is a desert, baked by the summer sun.
My body is a desert, swept dry by the autumn wind.
My body is a desert, frozen to ice beneath the winter sky.
No matter where I turn or what I try, a chill fills my wintry nights.
And I cry. And I cry.

He lies there for the rest of the hour, sobbing and staring up at the fluorescent lights.

Buy a bouquet of roses, the therapist suggests as he ushers him out, quickly locking the door behind him.

The patient departs. He has no faith in roses, but he buys roses. He not only buys roses, he buys an entire florist shop. He fills his car, his home, and his office with roses. And he is cured!

A sudden warmth flows from his toes and rises up to his brain. He becomes a fountain of joy. Everyone can see that he is changed.

When he walks the streets, women call out his name. Women follow him into alleys and bars and hotels. And such women! Never has he known women like these: woman with yellow hair and creamy legs and lips, women with soft hips and extra-large breasts, women who turn on as easily as lights with a switch. He has never lived the life of ready-made bliss!

One day he returns to the therapist on Chagrin Boulevard and offers him a bouquet of roses. *You saved my life!* he says, and he wraps his arms around the doctor and kisses him hard on the mouth. *You and your roses! At last I know the secret of life!* He leaves briskly without a backward glance.

No sooner is he gone, then the therapist begins to shiver. A chill fills the office, and the roses wilt, leaving a small puddle of petals on the carpeted floor. *I feel so cold,* the therapist moans. *I feel all alone in the universe.* He lies down on his couch, imagining some terrible flu has taken hold of him.

Soon his day turns into night, then night into day. No one calls. No one drops in. *Please, oh please,* the therapist says, *Why am I so cold? So alone? Is there no warmth left in this world?* One day he sits up to scribble a poem on a prescription pad, for only a poem can explain the despair he feels.

My body is a cold rock like a moon on an autumn night, he writes.
My body is a cold rock like a comet, spinning far from the light.
My body is a cold rock, all alone, in the dark lake of a thousand winter
nights.

He stares up at the ceiling light, tears sprouting from his eyes.

No matter where I turn or what I do, I am just a man in a cold, cold life.

Evidence
~ Rae Armantrout

Brittle, elevated
track

a snail laid down
on that flagstone,

its mysterious swerves.

*

When the cup tilts,
my eye appears
at the bottom,

placid, singular.

*

I've "added a window
to the world."

Believe it?

Look at these
convincing shards.

*

The flagstone
itself,

a jagged blue-
pink dawn

slab

So

~ Rae Armantrout

So that nothing
rhymes with much—

or starts to
and thinks better of it.

*

Ending with "like"
or "so."

Ending with "as if"

*

Virtual particles
carry the current

The Field: In the Heat of Winter
~ translated by Alex Cigale

to Rene Char

God-bonfire!—this pristine field
letting everything penetrate (and the mile posts
and the wind and the distant dots
of the windmills: progressing—as though away from
this world—imperceptibly—
slowly fleeing: oh all this
sparks—without tearing the flame
of the beyond-the-world bonfire)
what is—with no trace of even the worst
the shinning beyond-universe
God-bonfire

ПОЛЕ: В РАЗГАРЕ ЗИМЫ

~ original by Gennady Aygi

Рене Шару

бого-костер!—это чистое поле
все пропуская насквозь (и столбы верстовые
и ветер и точки далекие
мельниц: все более—будто из
этого мира—как не наяву—
удаляющиеся: о все это—
искры—не рвущие пламя
костра не-вселенского)
есмь—без следов от чего бы то ни было
не по-вселенски сияющий
бого-костер

(1970)

A Dream: Manuscripts

~ translated by Alex Cigale

*... une immense douleur a chaque page ...**
—Lautréamont. From a letter

Emerging out of the Sun—
you are contained in spirit, white!—

in forests,
from within illuminated:

by young maidens' dances!
and in this our time
that is not-ours

home fires scattered:
and the heart—among them

June 12, 1965

*The immense suffering of each page. (Fr.)

"The Field: In the Heat of Winter" and "A Dream: Manuscripts" are from Gennady Aygi's book *Fields in the City, Pages to France.*

СОН: РУКОПИСИ

~ original by Gennady Aygi

*... une immense douleur a chaque page ...**
—Lautréamont. Из письма

Выходящий из Солнца—
в духах содержишься белый!—

в лесах
изнутри озаряемых:

играми девичьими!—
и во времени этом
не-нашем

огни рассыпаны:
и сердце—в их числе

12 июня 1965

Огромная боль на каждой странице. Лотреамон (франц.)

Lesson of Reconnected Events

~ Angela Ball

Sister: *If the pony bucks you off, you must get back on.*

After four times, she let herself stay off. Since then she has tried to
stay off,
But others push her back on. In this way, she has traveled a
measurable distance
Downward.

Sister: *Don't wear white—it exhibits the dirt.*

Nothing she is has been well concealed, whatever her garment.

Husband: *You may remain in the dusty rear.*

Would sooner have the scenery unobscured by heaving and panting.

Sister: *Always keep one foot on the floor.*

Someone kissed her underwater but her eyes were open so that she
could see the people standing at the edge of the pool.

Dry friction resists relative lateral motion of two solid surfaces in contact.
Dry friction is subdivided into static friction between non-moving
surfaces,
And kinetic friction between moving surfaces.
Most instances are considered reconnected events.

In the Meantime

- JT Barbarese

I caress the parts I can reach safely,
and hold referenda in the smoke-filled
rooms of my hypnogogia, and half-asleep
see things that aren't there. The cup-stained table
where I worked and which I built, long trashed,
my son asleep on his crossed arms, Spanish money,
the phone number on a lost sticky, a 215 exchange,
a solar watermark on clouds, afterimages
of remembered lovers. Dumpster-diving in visions.
So much to go through. The take-out seems to be moving.

Will I be in the line for the movie about us, I
keep asking. Will I ever get over your beauty,
peel you from my words. In the meantime
I leave reality as is—unplowed, snowed-in,
idyllic and Swiss, a cabin, revealed slowly, squinting
from a painting of a similar cabin in the idyllic one,
one idyll containing another—far wall,
above the unlit stove where a kettle sits, idle.
Cold bronze blaze, or blaze of cold bronze?
This is not indecision, but longing. I light it,
hear the match scrape and pop and hear you a room away
like some form come to dwell among men
knowing the world won't underwrite the expenses.
The saints are manning phone-banks in the clouds,
they came on suddenly, inverting the picture, but
friends on the ground are whistling classic rock tunes,
and the wind rattles the road-kill, rib by rib.
The battered duck blind lisps prophecies,
the vultures are vulching—cool black miniature Zorros.
They delight me like good metaphors, earth-spring,
rapacious and caped toreadors. They peel and part

bone from furred flesh, then they look around,
monocular, like Bond villains, as if to say
maybe it's me, but I'll wait,
my imaginary friends will take care of this, make ends
fit means,
but I'd better wait, they are not here yet.

Please Don't Sell the Ferrari

~ Robin Behn

For the Brylcream smell is from my flying dream.

For there are no cupholders so we must drink the air.

For the wipers are shredded buffalo hide and the rollbar doesn't exist.

For it was forged long ago in the furnace where the top was pried off
the earth.

For my hair, flying, and your hair, flying, make a twisted rope the air
can climb.

For the passenger door handle is frozen like grim fate but my right hip
flexor leaps gazelle-like over the edge.

For the 5K we'd get for it would fix my tooth so well it would be all
that's left of me in the afterlife but I'd rather go toothless into
the wind.

For our ineptitude deserves a parade lap.

For the road begged me to beg you.

For my flying dream gets better mileage than your flying dream.

For the dogs nap in it.

For the surgeon you bought it from drove the blood off his hands in it.

For the interior is buttery maroon.

For it has a back seat anyone's past life can stretch out in.

For the recent ice age provides the A/C.

For the tape deck whirs and flips and bows to the thieves of music.

For I know a secret garage that matches your secret garage.

For the clutch is the clutch of ruination but you are my antenae's
little flag.

For the original inhabitants are toast but their shell remains, a
glittering tomb.

For the gas tank's aswirl with glittering bone flecks

of the dinosaur revving up his big boy dream.

To Market
- Sophie Cabot Black

Every day we eat as if not coming
Back. And each time I understand,
It turns into something else. To claim

The information was always there
Is masterful. The aisle is walked
And for each decision made, another

Unmakes. Haunts, as even with one look
It will come home with you. Everything open, nothing
Closed, all lights on. How capable we tell

Each other. From the start we were
Headed toward loss; we eat as if we might
Run out. When asked what it would mean to be

Done with not enough she could only see the end
Of beautiful. Of what it meant to cover.

"Facesti come quei che va di notte…"
~ translated by Hoyt Rogers

He brandished a peculiar torch:
Its double gleam perplexed the souls
Who groped along behind him,
Striving not to fear the abyss.

Guide, why have you never shone
On your own body the light you hold?
Have you no need to see the cleft
That opens up beneath your steps?

But such is allegory's fate: its deviser
Never knows, and must not know, where
His words arise, and where they fall.

His foot seeks toeholds in the void.
His flights of speech veer and quake,
Like flames more dreamless than ash.

« *Facesti come quei che va di notte…* »
~ original by Yves Bonnefoy

Il agitait une sorte de torche
Dont la double lueur déconcertait
Ces autres qui cherchaient derrière lui
À ne pas avoir peur, le long du gouffre.

Guide, pourquoi n'as-tu, sur ton propre corps,
Rien de cette lumière que tu offres ?
N'as-tu aucun besoin de percevoir
Le vide qui se creuse sous tes pas ?

Mais tel est le destin de l'allégorie :
Qui parle ne pourra ni ne doit savoir
D'où vient et où s'abîme sa parole.

Son pied cherche le sol à même le vide,
Son vol hésite et vire dans ses mots,
Flamme de moins de rêve que la cendre.

The Mocking of Ceres
~ translated by Hoyt Rogers

Trying to befriend his fever's words,
He peered through the clouded glass
Of his sleep. Outside, he heard talking.
He cracked the door: darkness, night...

Painter, whose hand is this you hold
While you sleep? Why not let go?
Can clinging to the hand of a child
Save you from the unrelenting fear

That blights your images? I dream
You will guide his trust to Ceres, who judges,
But also suffers; condemns, but also loves.

I dream you will make peace between desire
And the child: so his bafflement will cease,
And desire no longer lead him to his doom.

La dérision de Cérès
~ original by Yves Bonnefoy

Par amitié pour les mots de sa fièvre
Il regarda par la vitre embuée
De son sommeil. On se parlait, dehors,
Il entrouvrit sa porte, il faisait nuit.

Ah, peintre, qu'est-ce donc que cette main
Que tu prends dans la tienne quand tu dors,
Pourquoi la retiens-tu, cette main d'enfant,
Comme si sa pression te délivrait

D'une peur qui ravage tes images?
Moi, je rêve que tu en guides la confiance,
Jusqu'à celle qui juge, qui condamne,

Mais qui aime, et qui souffre. Que tu réconcilies
L'enfant et le désir. Qu'il n'y ait plus
D'étonnement dans l'un, de vindicte dans l'autre.

Rock Shrimp

~ Daniel Bosch

As a mantilla-clad widow
Backs into any
Pew to count, on bead castanets,
Decades of sorrow,

So, introvert, though distracted
By the hum of the aquarium
And by your swimmerets'
Attention to your roe,

The awarding of merits and demerits,
The binding and letting go,
Your withdrawal into the cleft
Yet betrays a forward impulse,

For they trawl, the cadmium insults,
The booms and masts and nets
Of your antennae,
Which cannot—quite—be retracted.

In Memory of Johnny Cash (1932-2003)

~ Daniel Bosch

At the end of the world I'll be
Nailing Jesus's hand to the tree
With a bright common sin
I have time to drive in
Before His blood sanctifies me.

Before Long

~ Christopher Buckley

> You must grieve for this right now
> you have to feel this sorrow now—
> for the world must be loved this much
> if you're going to say "I lived" . . .
> —Nazim Hikmet

Here's the thing . . .
4 billion years from now
the Andromeda Galaxy
and the Milky Way
are going to collide.
In 2012,
Hubble Space Telescope
researchers concluded
the collision is definite,
and, there's a 50% chance
our solar system will be swept
three times farther out from
the galactic core than it is
today.
Andromeda has crashed
into at least one other galaxy,
and several dwarf galaxies
are plowing into the Milky Way
right now, but not every star
will collide—
there are distances. . . .
The analogy comes out to one
ping-pong ball every mile or so—
more integration and stellar drive-by
than obliteration.
Either way,

by the time it all bangs up,
all the water on the surface
of the earth will have boiled away
from the increasing luminosity
of the sun, thereby ending
terrestrial life . . .
                                        that's due
in only about 1.4 billion years,
nothing, really, in relation
to the cosmic spread sheet
of time, the algorithm of the dark,
but nothing, finally, all the same . . .
a 1-2-punch for our forthcoming end
the scientists blithely report—
and they're good with that?
                                                        I feel
like that character in Woody Allen's
Stardust Memories who obsesses
about the *New York Times* article
on matter decaying, the universe
gradually breaking down and how
there's not going to be anything left—
"Am I the only one that saw that?"
he asks. And though the science is dated
now, that deep sense of urgency
and dread obtains.
                                        The great Hikmet,
writing by the Sea of Azov
in the early '60s admonished us
on living—
                        how we must mourn
for the future, or lack thereof,
right now, before the scalded rock
of our planet is released into
the black & white silence of space

without fanfare or a molecule
of moisture left. Last year
the Sea of Azov turned blood-red
near the village of Berdyansk;
older locals warned it was
a sign of coming events.
Hikmet admired the stars,
their winsome, their wondrous
mystery, but he was no
soothsayer, no astrologer;
his rustic soul was rooted
in the soil.
                    So where is Hikmet
now, and where is the dear soul
of my mother? And what about
the flow chart of light?
Even the skeptical
don't want to give up thinking
there might be a reservoir
of souls spinning along
with us, mist-like, moon-like,
circling this blue fleck
in the anterooms of the dark.
Even over-compensated
athletes point up to the sky
as if a God were standing
on a terrace of clouds
apportioning lavish rewards
and endorsements for touchdowns
and walk-off home runs, though
they are, as a group, light years from
metaphysicians or cosmologists
who know that there is no "up" out there,
that the galaxies are tilted, tossed out
catywampus in mostly unfilled space,

only 4% of it anything at all
in the Standard Model now.
But for a moment they feel
immortal.
                    No way to know.
As a child, I was content
in my little school on the hill
in back of town. I'd race to the swings
and pump my legs, climbing high
into the immediate bowl
of space humming, "Wonderful,
Wonderful Copenhagen, Wonderful
By the Sea"—a song I'd heard
in a movie about a man who wrote
fairy tales for children, and, as I lived
by the sea, which was wonderful
and pure in 1953, it made sense to me,
and for the time being I took the music
and the story on faith, I took the sky,
singing away there, lifting into the air,
mornings and afternoons,
everything then rotating so slowly
about me, so far away, that I was sure
I was a life source as much as
the first stars coming up, though
my feet touched down heading home
each day, firmly, forever on the earth.

Carmina, 13
~ translated by Len Krisak

At my place—soon, Fabullus—you'll have dined
Deliciously. That's *if* the gods are kind
To you and *if* you bring good food along . . .
And plenty of it. Don't forget a charming
Girl either, or your wine and wit and song
Like laughter. Bring me everything disarming,
Friend, and you'll dine well. You could do worse,
For spiders have been stringing in my purse.
But come, and in return, accept love neat, or
Something even finer, even sweeter:
For I'll give you a perfume so refined—
A gift the Venuses and Cupids chose
To give my girl—that when you smell its rose,
Fabullus, you'll pray you were one great nose.

~ original by Catullus

Cenabis bene, mi Fabulle, apud me
paucis, si tibi di fauent, diebus,
si tecum attuleris bonam atque magnam
cenam, non sine candida puella
et uino et sale et omnibus cachinnis.
haec si, inquam, attuleris, uenuste noster,
cenabis bene; nam tui Catulli
plenus sacculus est aranearum.
sed contra accipies meros amores
seu quid suauius elegantiusue est:
nam unguentum dabo, quod meae puellae
donarunt Veneres Cupidinesque,
quod tu cum olfacies, deos rogabis,
totum ut te faciant, Fabulle, nasum.

FROM BLIND DISTANCE
~ translated by John Taylor

The Opposite of Insomnia

In the depths *(so motionless one's ears prick up)*, in the very depths of night a clearing opens. *(My sleep, this tower.)* I awake as if at the heart of a pinewood. Uncertain and peaceful *(perhaps a noise)*, unheard-of, shrill *(or when I approach?)*, whimsical, monotonous *(thin blades)*, lighthearted and free, and nonetheless ever led back to the same twirling *(this thread on which I depend)*, to the same halts above emptiness *(constantly snaps again wherever tied back together)*, the sound of a flute rises all the way up to my silent room. *(My dream, this fragrance.)*

The First Image

Fleeing in all directions, fur shiny in the sunlight, the sprawled-out dog, silent foxhunt! *(No, no: simply chasing as a game, the same sequence ever repeated.)* Yet, first, the field of light! The flies buzzing around me are drilling chasms into it that close up just as soon. Awakening *(the stinging wind, tiny embers on the skin)*; momentum *(both absorbed in the motley colored meadows on the hill across from me and ceaselessly scouring the countryside)*; waiting *(motionless like a fixed point in the joyous free-for-all)*. The scattered shadow of one cloud, then another *(groping like a wandering hand)*, is slowly gliding along, and the first image comes back whole; will soon come back, again welling like a source.

Like the Summer

What place, what room without walls is never crossed nor occupied by anything, not even coolness? I am only drifting, immersed in luminous water, the same limit never gone beyond. Bound I am by voices coming up from below, now silent—friendly or not, joyous, fraternal, transparent as well like the summer about to surge forth in the depths, in the uttermost depths of night, and like impossible bursts of laughter.

Late Fall

Emerges just in time, hollowed out, striped with shadow and glimmering *(the rows of espaliered trees, the panes of window frames)*, as if raised above the mist-covered greenhouse *(aerostat, hot-air balloon of November)*, the hillside clouded over at the top by an orchard of trees that are already black, in front of the leafless other ones, except for an apple tree still covered with its fruit. Chinese lanterns of a party now over, paled gleams that the sun revives by melting the frost deposited at night on their redness.

The Balance of the Daylight

Brought back to this level path, I am walking by an orchard at the limit of the fog. Laundry hanging between trees; a crumbled-down wall that no longer encloses. Below, as if hatching, the noise of cars driving through the cluse. Higher up, a dazzling birdsong. I think I am touching, I am indeed touching the screen of the light, the espalier, the facade whose top is perhaps already gleaming. No more village despite the background noise, despite gonglike hammering on a piece of sheet metal. Pathless, I proceed; on this path running past the houses, the only street, among the frosty pastures, running past the gray wall of the morning, among the plowed fields—night pulled back down against the ground and turned over. In the thundering sunlight, the bird alights on the roof.

"Blind Distance" is the title sequence of the book *Distance aveugle*, Paris: José Corti, 2000.

FROM *DISTANCE AVEUGLE*
~ original by Pierre Chappuis

Le contraire d'une insomnie

Au fond *(immobile, à tendre l'oreille)*, tout au fond de la nuit s'ouvre une clairière. *(Mon sommeil, cette tour.)* Je m'éveille comme au cœur d'une pinède. Incertain et paisible *(peut-être un bruit)*, inouï, aigu *(ou je m'approche)*, capricieux, monotone *(de minces lames)*, léger et libre, et cependant toujours ramené aux mêmes virevoltes *(ce fil dont je dépends)*, aux mêmes stations au-dessus du vide *(se rompt sans cesse, n'importe où se renoue)*, le chant d'une flûte s'élève jusqu'à ma chambre de silence. *(Mon rêve, ce parfum.)*

L'image première

Fuite en tous sens, pelage lustré par le soleil, chien couché, chasse à courre muette ! *(Non, non : simple poursuite, par jeu, la même séquence toujours répétée.)* Mais, d'abord, le champ de la lumière ! Les mouches bourdonnant autour de moi y forent des gouffres refermés aussitôt. Éveil *(le picotement du vent, petites braises sur la peau)* ; élan *(à la fois tout à la bigarrure des prés sur la colline en face de moi, et battant le pays sans relâche)* ; attente *(immobile comme un point fixe dans l'heureuse mêlée)*. Lentement glisse, éparse, l'ombre d'un nuage, puis d'un autre *(tâtonnement comme d'une main égarée)* et l'image première, une, revient ; reviendra bientôt, refera source.

Comme l'été

Quel lieu, quelle chambre sans murs que rien ne traverse ou n'habite ni même la fraîcheur ? Je dérive seulement, plongé dans une eau lumineuse, la même limite jamais franchie. Me lient, venues d'en bas, des voix maintenant tues, amies ou non, joyeuses, fraternelles, transparentes elles aussi comme l'été à jaillir au fond, tout au fond de la nuit, et d'impossibles éclats de rire.

Arrière-saison

À temps surgit, évidé, strié d'ombre et de luisances *(les rangées d'espaliers, les vitres des châssis)*, comme élevé au-dessus de la serre embuée *(aérostat, montgolfière de novembre)*, le coteau qu'ennuage en son sommet un verger aux arbres déjà noirs sauf, en avant des autres, toutes feuilles tombées, un pommier encore couvert de ses fruits. Lampions d'une fête passée, lueurs pâlies que le soleil ravive en faisant fondre le gel déposé nuitamment sur leur rouge.

La balance du jour

Ramené sur ce chemin horizontal, je longe un verger à la limite du brouillard. Lessive suspendue entre les arbres ; mur effrité, qui n'enclôt. Au-dessous, comme couvé, le bruit des voitures qui passent dans la cluse. Plus haut, éclatant, un chant d'oiseau. Je crois toucher, je touche l'écran de la lumière, l'espalier, la façade dont le sommet resplendit peut-être déjà. Plus de village, malgré la rumeur, malgré les coups de gong d'un marteau sur une plaque de tôle. Sans chemin, je vais ; sur ce chemin, longeant les maisons, l'unique rue, parmi les pâtis couverts de gelée blanche, longeant le mur gris du matin, parmi les champs labourés — nuit rabattue contre le sol, retournée sur elle-même. Dans le soleil tonitruant, l'oiseau se pose sur le toit.

Clark

~ Patricia Clark

after Weldon Kees

The maintenance man calls himself Fred,
calls these buildings "suds" because as Clark notes down
the laundry women lived here, washing clothes,
and more, for the officers on the base.

"Where's the shutoff valve?"—but no one knows.
Fred will check a map; Clark drives away.
The music tears a ragged hole into her heart.

When the battleship-gray clouds match walls
someone better go out, go dance and forget.
There are maps in the car, sand on the floor.
There's a coastline eroding with the tide, so go.

Flowers to buy: no more pale tulips, but blooms
like dahlias, spiky, nodding, in neon
shades of red, purple, gold. "Tender" the word

for dahlias, Clark recalls from the green-thumb
woman—her mother, if the name be known.

Outside, the birds crank up cries like jazz.
Outside, the four suds buildings make a square.
Where the bay glints pewter and takes no prisoner.

Ars Polis

~ Andrei Codrescu

the frequency of portraits in post-mortem inventories
in the 17th to the 18th century grows from 18 to 28 percent
while the percentage of religious portraits falls from 29 to 12 percent
—George Vigarello

way too human too fast way too boring too quick
the wrong humans at that
humans that tick like clocks
the saints were in no hurry
nor the poor
every time a slum is being abolished
peoples' right to get fucked up
is abridged
more immortality ground up like beef
display patties in square windows
no streets to perform on
no place to squat for a good shell game
OTB poetry parlor where are you?
poetry that good superstition
guessing where the third pea hides
anybody can play
you can't be a bit superstitious
and a bit rational
a little in a book and a little outside
but you can keep betting
and never guessing
and when they explain everything on tv
Japanese woman arrested for killing virtual husband
on the crawl that used to be the street
you walk three frustrated miles
meeting no one you know no one who knows you
you could swear it's the same place where you had

hundreds of friends and acquintances
the buildings haven't moved
you never find out where the party is

The gaze doesn't reveal anything
it places us instantly in a different situation
(Victor Brauner)
no point in looking for it
it's not the past or the wrong city
it's your transparent body
Sola la muerte es fuerte

Frank O'Hara's Golden Gondola

~ Andrea Cohen

It never really belonged
to Frank, or should I say,
Mr. O'Hara. He stashed it
in the pocket of his white
linen jacket after bantering, after
buying the trinket from a merchant
of gilded kitsch on the Rialto,
and presented it, not
to his lover, Bill, but to
his young friend Lise, as the three
drifted in a larger golden gondola
beneath the Bridge of Sighs. She
was the daughter of a painter
Frank was not. Like her father,
she liked Frank a lot, but more
than Frank, she adored Bill, his lover, and held
out hope that Frank's gift beneath
the Bridge of Sighs signified a rift
between Bill and Frank, a narrows
through which she and Bill might
slip into Venetian bliss. A girl,
at ten, dreams like this. She considers
everything, the way Frank
O'Hara did in his lunch-time walks, in
his conveyance of "The Day Lady Died."
While Lise and Bill and Frank, guided
by a lithe gondolier making eyes
at Frank and Bill, drifted down
the canal, Frank would have mentioned
Byron, how he coined the phrase
The Bridge of Sighs, imagining the convicts,
prison-led, getting their last glimpse

of the City of Masks. In fact,
Venice was visible from the prison, which
must have tormented the prisoners more,
the way it's torture to ride in a gondola
with your secret love nuzzling his lover.
The girl of ten lugged the golden gondola
across the years of rooms, until a roommate
in Key West pilfered it, and the gondola
with its flaking, gold paint got passed
like a party girl from stranger to stranger,
enlisted as paper-weight, as door-stop, as
the blunt instrument a memento
of the City of Bridges, cast out, becomes.

Cool to the Touch

- Billy Collins

was how my metal razor felt
one autumn morning in New Hampshire,
a sign that the season was shifting
from the ease of gold to the bite of steel.

I had been warm in my bed
while the room and its things cooled
in the night air that flowed
over the sills of the open windows.

And cool was the edge of the white sink
and the silvery faucet bearing the letter C
for fall was tumbling into winter now
and yellow leaves were loosening around the house.

So this is how it's going to be
I thought as I stood before the mirror,
my face white with suds
my warm body alert to the chill of the world.

Postscript

~ Martha Collins

What if we'd known that Africa
was the home of us all, of all people:

those who settled their own continent,
those who crossing the Red Sea trekked

through the Middle East into Asia,
those who later went south to Australia,

those who still later, after the warming,
went north to Europe and lost their color,

and finally those who went farther east
across the Strait into North America,

traveling on to the south, and east,
where I am thinking of those who stayed

and their distant ancestors, also ours,
who gave us our human lives—?

FROM OF MARRIAGE: A SEQUENCE

~ Nicole Cooley

Marriage as a Bank of Snow Shaved Flat

What would weld us together now—a slap?

White print of a hand on a face.
Skate blade in a sharpener.
Snow soaking up light.

Marriage as Yellow Umbrella

You inch my zipper down my back, teeth caught:
rip of silk, rip of plastic, rip of skin.
Body that's been opened up already twice.

Marriage as Chinese Jump Rope

Red and black twined rubber band binding
two girls on the playground together—
turn and flip and twist.
Pull the elastic around my ankles tight.
You don't know what I'm talking about, do you?

Marriage as the Poem

I tore the poem
into tiny pieces, slipped them in
the envelope, tongued it shut,
crushed it between
our mattress and the box spring
of our bed.

Marriage as the Breakfast Menu at La Habana

Divorced Eggs: one with red sauce, one with salsa verde.
Beside each other, side by side, like breasts on a plate.

Marriage as C Train to Brooklyn

Beside me the man bites the hospital bracelet off the woman's wrist,
tears white plastic tape off with his teeth.

Marriage as a Plate of Spinach

Leaves bottle green as a dress, the wrong dress,
the one you took from my closet,
let fall over my shoulders to the floor.
Leave it there.
Don't pick it up.
All bitter lace.
In my favorite fairy tale all the bad mother desires
is sharp-leaved rampion.
She gives up her first child.
I said drop the dress right now.
Come here.

A Poem About Your Body

~ Peter Cooley

"The Holy Family" by Michelangelo

Renaissance weather, sultry, sun-drenched
drove this Christ the baby to strip off his clothes.
Here, the entire composition, Mary's gaze and Joseph's,
suspends the little one in space of the divine
driving toward His penis.
                                        If you wonder about Jesus,
how he could get away acting lunatic, shouting
"I came to bring fire to the earth and how I wish it were already
            kindled"
and yet be one of us, examine here the chubby little body
you and I began with.
                                        Michaelangelo, though,
has lit the skin within along the biceps and upper calves
muscles where leg meets thigh. That he was bi-sexual
gave him, no doubt, a double vision of the body
redoubled that it be human and divine. And so it is
God came naked to us as ourselves.

Port Dreams

~ Josh Cook

Gulls plummet from

clouds that look like stretched steel wool.

Ocean spray is the color of ashes.

There are all also the brusque shouts of longshoremen, slowly

losing the war of attrition against cargo piled in their ports.

I got myself into a boat last night.

The tide knocked my dinghy on a pier post,

The photo-booth photos in my pocket

proved I was attracted to her fashion not her person.

A pocket pat finds the stud she had in her labre.

Now she's got nothing going for her.

I stretch my legs

and kick a layer of crap at the bottom of the dinghy;

a canteen,

a box of safety matches,

a first aid kit,

half the shit I'd take with me to a deserted island.

Even Lolita.

The bar was late. The night was smoky.

I was looking for a port storm or not.

Her codes matched my mood;

I wanted to get laid

and guessed she went for literate men.

So, I steered the conversation towards Querelle.

The smell of the ocean like a hungry child on the last errand.

It made her think I was gay.

"And?"

"We talked all night long, lying on the beach while longshoremen
sold drugs around us; bums built houses from drift
wood, teenagers found bonfires on fire, surfers mailed
postcards, and seals squawked at reluctant rowers; the
last lighthousekeeper searched for his contacts in the
sand, the police passed cursory searchlights over the sand,
the journalists slowly tore single pages from their final
notebooks; and the mainstreet of the quainttown downtown
coastal village remained a postern for ghosts escaping inland.

I left with the tide

coming in while she was asleep."

The world rocks instead of spins,

all of us seasick sitting in the middle,

hanging on to

whatever,

whatever,

whatever,

we can.

Wrestling with the bulky life-jackets, failing to strangle the straps and clasps, blushing at how the yellow clashes with the red tie we finally had the guts to wear,

we barely notice that ashes have mixed with the oceanspray,

so the conclusion bobs a few inches from our fingers until.

The seabirds distract us,

cycling through synonyms for "to plummet."

Monody with a Line from Rupert Brooke

~ Brian Culhane

It's only the wind tapping on the pane.
No words, nothing whispered, no news.
They say that the Dead die not, but remain.

Boulevards glisten in freezing rain.
Back and forth, walk ones and twos.
It's only the wind tapping on the pane.

The dog looks up from where she's lain:
A screech crisscrosses slick avenues.
They say that the Dead die not, but remain.

But what can the living hope to gain?
Hear that sound? The scuffle of shoes!
Oh, only the wind tapping on the pane.

Sleet and more sleet: tonight's refrain,
A sound no one willingly would choose.
They say that the Dead die not, but remain.

The dog whimpers over and over again.
No words. Nothing whispered. No news.
They say that the Dead die not, but remain.
It's only the wind tapping on the pane.

The New Math

- Jim Daniels

On the basement futon, my daughter
squeezes my hand through yet
another kids' movie killing off the dad
which prompts a long conversation
in which tallies are taken, dead mothers
vs. dead fathers. Nothing happens
if the parents stick around.
I've been writing the new year on my checks,
and I don't like it. *Damn* is acceptable
in children's films, but not *shit. Hell?* Yes.
Yet try explaining limbo to a seven-year-old.
Like a bowling ball rolling down one endless alley,
the kiddie bumpers up, so you can't throw
a gutter ball. Their real dads are sitting back
raking in the dough their kids make *acting*!
I'm developing a fondness for the exclamation
point! Look kids, I'm not sleeping! I'm not tired!
Just because God isn't talking to you and me
doesn't mean he's not out there keeping score.
Shucks, I'm back in a Western again. Somebody
has to be the sheriff's kids, and I'm deputizing
you and you. When I was a kid, we didn't have
futons or DVDs. But we had guardian angels
and undisputed national champions.
Okay, your dad's a fibber. But say the moon
is your bowling ball, wouldn't you want to just grab it
and hold on? I'm gonna die, regardless of my grammar.
Just like in the movies. And you'll have
some great adventure called the rest of your life.
Me, I'll be popcorn stars and bad reception.
When you're lying in bed late at night,
whisper to me the latest new things.

Animal Husbandry

~ Carl Dennis

Isn't it time to mention the billions
Of animal innocents allowed to drown
In the story of Noah, the billions sacrificed
As collateral damage when Jahweh decides
To drown mankind? Can so gross an act of injustice
Be allowed to pass without an apology?
The next edition should at least contain a chapter
On what felt it felt like for Noah and family
To enter, when the flood receded, a world
Of empty fields and forests, of empty sky.
And then a longer chapter on the remnant pairs
Returning to habitats devoid of their kin,
The strain of two bees trying to be a hive,
Two prairie dogs toiling to be a colony.
And consider the loneliness of the dove
Sent from the ark to scout for land,
As it waited in the reeds for the ark to open.
Then imagine it darting off with its mate,
Quick to put as much distance as possible
Between them and Noah's family.
Who knows when the god of humans
Might strike out blindly again in all directions,
As if the world were to blame for his failure,
On the sixth day of creation, to plan
The last two creatures as carefully
As he planned the others. And then his failure
To observe them at least a year in the Garden
Before he urged them to fill the world.

Hayes Street Evening Fugue

- W.S. Di Piero

Suppenküche. Babies. Zonal. Citizen Cake.
Upstairs: inept blues amped; a silhouette at a drawing board;
a blacked-out window; jeans and socks on a line.
What happens in those rooms? Everybody's a secret
with a secret. The light diminishes them. A photo hound
deploys draperies and shades. Looming lingerie
fills with flesh. A woman in pajamas spins with love
that's pure deception but all she can know.
Next door, a baby girl's face, slicked with mucus,
pastes itself to a window while Buxtehude
(who offers Bach his post if he weds the daughter:
Bach says no, oh no) exalts through those rooms
that are organ pipes announcing heaven on earth,
and behind the sickly child's face the mother weaves,
and it's Aphrodite, her again, apparitional in the weave,
caretaking those who love and live one story up.

(Often he tried to imagine...)

- Stephen Dobyns

Often he tried to imagine the intimacy enjoyed by others, friendships of telepathic closeness, families bound lovingly like families in old movies—the parents caring, the children happy. And those groups of people picnicking in parks as he walked by on a path beneath the trees, or groups laughing together in restaurants—he pictured friends growing up together, being the support of one another through full lives, and then their funerals with long lines of automobiles traveling slowly with their lights on. He never thought these people might experience anxiety or doubt, that dark uncertainty could fill them with dread, that ambition or envy might lead them to compromise whatever ideals they had at the start. In fact, he never thought they might be like he was. Yet if he had, if he'd seen in others his own image, wouldn't his isolation have been decreased? If fear hadn't blurred his vision of the world, wouldn't he have found that he too had a place within it?

Throne Verse
~ Patrick Donnelly

Two years of cinders built up in the hearth,
the new over and over the old.

I'd made nothing for months, just consumed
or operated what others made.

Pointless to say what, but I will: frozen food,
my name on petitions to save various things,

a spray for scale on the plants,
films that streamed to me from a link,

sometimes viewed from our bed, which
either went unmade or was made so particularly

as the only task I could complete all day
that I would not let my love help

and accused him
of not knowing how.

Before this, I'd made an effort, sent it out
for judgment and could make nothing else till I heard.

But did I have to compare every breath I drew
to "an angioplasty"?

Did I have to be so sad?
Did I have to be as sad as my mother had been sad

and in the same way,
and hadn't I lectured her before she went

not to make her sadness a burden for others,
and by others hadn't I meant me?

A job of work was what had vexed me,
three years, or eight years, or fifty-four, depending.

The time might have wished to release to me
some money or some other boon,

but not right there or then,
the hour wasn't right. So those things collected upriver

behind some kind of dam,
like jellies in a larder, jars of garnets I couldn't lift from the water,

garnets from Kenya, Finland, Rajasthan, the Ural Mountains,
pomegranates, gooseberries, stones made of cinnamon, live coals.

Are you the type of person who doesn't need approval?

Who keeps on working, no matter what?
Like God, whose throne, it is written, extends

over the heavens and the earth
and who "feels no fatigue in guarding and preserving them"?

Well, good for you—right now I don't care to lift
even the thinnest, netherest edge of the counterpane.

Nobody has yet said
we can't afford to hold up the whole Internet forever,

but that's right, don't you see? We'll have to vote
which parts to lose, which secret giant facilities

to keep cool with electricity made from burning coals.
Will it be the levels of games, the libraries, or the paths to the
lonesome

no-talking-no-kissing-no-reciprocating hook-ups?
That was the link from which I somehow met my love,

and now it's all gone—click there, if you don't believe.
Even the gate has disappeared, from when

America was Online. Now the young flood
along other routes, open to them alone.

Wasn't it two months before the crazy old girl died
that I wrote in a letter I must have sent

TO HER HOSPITAL BED, for Christ's sake,
that "the kindest thing anyone could do for others

is to face their own fears"? And didn't she reply
she was "not up to being challenged on any part

of her worldview right then"? Whatever happened
to her garnet wedding band? Sweet bloody prophets and saints,

at least I turned off the screens to write this,
several days running, at least I worked.

Just how long might you be inclined
to help me lift my heavy head

off its throne of heaped and burning dung?

The Worry of an Aerial Procession
~ Norman Dubie

(So think of it, but off the coastline,
up north,
while the orange and pink drone,
among the rented clouds, watches the children.

Look at the hillside wedding banquet—
sweet cheeses stacked
with a sweet paint, a mule
being beaten by the roadside,
chewed at like a long black pencil,
the large dog sunning himself
in the afternoon fog rolling over
a far rainstorm that's milling
among the whiter mountains.

The vaudeville ventriloquist says
the poem and novel are now
a dusty shop with a few dollars
in an old cigar box.

But borrow the naked eyeball
from a pyramid full of wig powder and place it
in the firewall of science
and you will win admission to the secret lotto
of the withdrawn dystopia-fraud
that Blake thought of as a dark open clause…

So, it's Apache Junction and Cave Creek
of which I speak, whose citizens
I've never met, they are
being swallowed by increasing debt
who yet somehow never borrowed

a single penny. And late in the round
they turn, who once
lifted the dark shovel in a fast drying mud
of an endless lament and call… they say,

the bureaucrat is the enemy of us all.

Bechdel Test (TAKE ONE)

~ Denise Duhamel

Maureen and Denise talk about their daughters and nieces, the best place for sushi, the yes/no game, *Cosmo* questionnaires, tarot cards, hallucinations, witchcraft, Kraft cheese, Ma Barker, Little Red, communism, the recession, the national debt, existential questions of blame, criminal blame, Tina Fey, *Parks and Recreation* (Denise has never seen it), recreational drug use, their mothers, the mother lode, dignity, degenerate eye disease, jewelry, fishing, flashing, Palestine, flotillas, tortillas, furniture and fashion, the death penalty, absolution, Absolut vodka, powerlessness, the power grid, the daily grind, ground pepper vs. peppercorn, footwear, cookware, Margaret Thatcher, their new smart phones, the weather (hurricanes), baked kale with sea salt, Björk, tort reform, compulsive truth-tellers, the wherewithal of women and girls.

Clauses After Verbs of Fearing

~ Angie Estes

She said, *Sometimes it's good to forget*
to remember: you can think it
but it doesn't make any sense—like the cortége

of names of 77, 297 Czech Jews
murdered in World War II that continues
to wind around the walls inside

the Pinkas Synagogue while the hands
of the old Town Hall's Hebrew clock keep
turning back. When St. John of Nepomuk

was thrown off the Charles Bridge
for refusing to divulge secrets
of the confessional, a cluster of stars

appeared over the spot in the river
where he drowned, but should my mother
become synonymous with epilogues

in Prague, there would be
no more stars—not for ships
that triangulate their way to ports

they've never glimpsed—and birds would have to
find their way with words to some distant leafing
branch. Before she slips from consciousness

like a slip of the tongue, becomes only
the shell of *she'll* or a camellia's
flushed cameo, consult the Latin grammar

on the use of clauses after verbs of
fearing: how to conjugate something that is
not wanted, as in *I fear*

lest she fail. Silhouette
is the hardest word in the English language
to spell because it is intentionally made

incomplete, something of ephemeral
value, and because it is not
English. It's so early, morning, the world's still

an x-ray clipped to my window
like the photograph I took of the stone pines
at night on the grounds of the Villa Aurelia, teased

and coiffed—a forest of brains—taken
on the grounds that we can't say
what darkness looks like

any other way: sweet as the hollow-stemmed
honeysuckle, sheen of gloss when
it can't remember its g.

My Correspondence with Wallace Stevens

~ Kathleen Flenniken

I addressed him
Grandmaster of Loneliness.

He confessed
to studying a blue smudge in one of his still lifes
for hours amounting to days.

Afternoon, late November,
I came across a field of snow
bordered by tangled chiaroscuro trees,

and my gratitude—.
But he—.

I observed
like a crow traversing a gun scope
my outsized need to be praised.

Everything else has been subterfuge.

Or so I inferred from the silence
he left as reply.

Planet Greece

- Tess Gallagher

He says, with mystification, they took a third
of his dead wife's pension, she who was so afraid
to lose her job she never told anyone
how tired, how depleted she felt as her blood
more and more refused to carry
her. Then one day she died, leaving their eight
children nearly grown. But she'd worked every day
and no one knew, but him, of course. He knew.

And her pension, which proved she had worked,
was now leaking out of her death and over to
the government which claimed it as his surplus,
money which had sustained him when work
was scarce—the faint signal of her life blinking now
like a worn-out star in the pocket of the state.
He is old and nearly finished with the journey.
How boldly they announce they will take a portion
of his own small pension next. What would he use it
for? Coal? A bit of meat? Seed for the birds?

Without leaving his hearth in Ireland he flies
through space with his country on his back. The place
he lands is rocky and chill just like his homeland.
He sits at his hearth in the middle of a field and
spirits rise up from the ground and the tiny hearths
of the stars take over the field of his mind. The slow
white ovens of the sheep come close. History and
governments whirl like planetary dust away
into the vastness of space. Coming in from the nightshift

at the mental home, she kisses him as they pass in the hall,
and, as in the days of their youth, she hands him,
like a small kingdom, the keys to the car.

Cabin Fever

~ Brendan Galvin

1.
That candidate whose face on TV
seemed a mattress abandoned
to his spirit's vacant lot
drove me out to the woodpile.

Breaking into rounds of cold oak,
trying not to think of meretricious
skulls, I gave up and set the axe aside,
and began listening to the grove

creaking here and there, the slight
groans and sighs of pitch pines and oaks,
the breeze weaving higher branches
together, locusts playing off one another,

a reasonable music, neither
electronic nor human, until a redbelly
began heckling from a pine crown,
a reminder to gather my splits

and build a fire in the stove before
the first flakes, to knot up Metro
and Sunday Styles before snow
oversimplified the paths and woodshed,

to attend the flames as though
back in a time when humanity
had little as companionable.

2.
The blizzard inside the hurricane,
or is it the hurricane inside the blizzard?
In all this banging and flapping
a god within another god has ordered

the spruces to bow down and peppered
these windows with salt spray. Can there be
an "I" in this storm surge rolling the coast
over until stumps of that ancient cedar swamp

appear briefly again, proof that the sea
when it's ready will take us back, as the air
and its waters took the cedar fenceposts back.
What of the juncos and nuthatches out there

exploring interstices of ice, the sparrows
and chickadees in their workaday coveralls.
The light dives for zero, and the clock
drips each second like a plumber's nightmare.

Time to consider how far those birds have flown
from *T. rex.* In the woodstove window a face
keeps appearing, almost familiar. We too
are made of carbon and flames.

Henry's Song

~ Beckian Fritz Goldberg

for Nancy and Bill

Sometimes sitting in a friend's backyard on a fall evening
a thing comes to you. But then you second guess yourself.
You second guess yourself, and your grace is gone.
The cat dish is there by the step, overturned in the dry leaves,
the trees here taller than any trees in your dreams. You're afraid
if you stay here they might talk. And these nights
you only want to hear someone say, *Yes,*
I think of these things too… Nine o'clock, cold,
I couldn't see the stars for the trees, only the yellow light
of the back window doubled over on the ground. In it,
leaves laid with the kitchen. Then a figure passed:
My friend reaching up into the cupboard and looking lost
a little while. His wife bringing in a cup and dish. Both of them
standing by the sink talking maybe about buying apples tomorrow
or what movie or the jacket no one can find. Her hair
was still damp from the shower and haloed in the kitchen light
as he crossed into the next room blue with the blink of the TV.
That afternoon my friend had thought his cat was lost and we
searched for an hour but the cat had sunk into a deep pile of leaves,
lay half-covered and asleep. The cat who was not lost was named
Henry and he was dead a few weeks later of old age. At night
he'd come in the room where I was slept and sit
staring down at the heating vent and, hours later, if I rose to pee,
he'd still be there as if waiting for something specific to rise
through the floor. But life inside the house that night was golden,
though then the kitchen was lonely, the cereal boxes misaligned
on the shelf, a nest of white bowls, mugs upside down in a row.
I thought someone will be left to open the cupboards after
we are dead and there see everything has stayed the way
we left it. Say yes, you think of these things too. And that's

when the thing that came to me came to me and when I
second guessed myself I lost what the thing was. Sometime
it might return, but for now I'll say it was nothing. It was nothing.
Inside the house someone was asking, Did you take Avantix
and suffer heart failure? Do you live alone? Are you tired of carpet
　　stains?
Do you need a loan fast? Yes. And yes and yes and yes.
I've thought of these things, too–standing at the window while
　　skeletons
on TV marched toward a cartoon cowboy. It was even stranger
in the silence of early November, away from home. But life was
　　gorgeous
in the house. The glazed red sugar bowl gleamed. Months
later, my friend told me sometimes he'd still mistake
the shadow, the wool scarf bunched on the chair, and think
it's Henry. As if the mind believed absence is a trick. For it
can still see everything. But the world asks, Do you have crow's feet?
Do you have enough to cover your funeral costs? Ever feel irregular?

Do you have trouble sleeping? That night the wind blowing
dead leaves sounded like a distant ocean, my fingertips
numbed with cold & the lit window held everything sacred
in its church. I saw that light the next day slanting as we walked
through an apple orchard and stopped at the mill for cider.
Farther on, we came to a large pond where pike and recluse sturgeon
lurked beneath the surface. On the bridge was a machine you'd put
a quarter in for a handful of food for the fish. I watched my friend
toss some in the water and the pond became alive with thrashing
bodies, the surface almost writhing with their gleams, the sound
of water laughing all around, and then they disappeared again,
the water like a shadow, deep, blue-green. And quiet. There was
a small breeze, an open field, a white clapboard building
on one side. Things are simple, that's what we forget.
When I slept that night I left the door ajar for Henry
who would come upstairs late for his vigil, the warm air

floating above the vent from some underworld
benevolent beyond his dreams. And when I woke later in the dark
as sometimes you do in a strange bed away from home
in a strange town with a moon and trees, I could feel he was there
long before I could distinguish his shape, before I could remember
exactly where I was. It came to me this loneliness is something we
take
with us anywhere and not that we aren't loved, but that we aren't
loved forever. Life demands much less. The fish is purely
fish and that's enough. An apple wholly apple. Maybe it's enough
to be human, leave the door open, wait for a soul–which, if it comes,
comes
like the half of the conversation we imagined because we
can't imagine that speaking is only speaking, even to the night,
the way we can't believe death is only death, the way we can't
stand outside a window on a fall evening in a pile of leaves in
Kalamazoo
and not count ourselves among the missing. Are you single and
looking
for your soul mate? Are you drowning in credit card debt?
Do you want more hair? Do you have trouble sleeping? Yes,
I have trouble sleeping. But, when it was my turn, I cupped my hand
and the machine filled it with food for the fish I scattered
over the water and they came like the rush of fat rain up
from the deep, glittering, swarming over nothing. It made me happy.
Then the green silence closing over them again. The little cat
waiting faithfully in the dark for his death and not complaining.
And us, knowing it is already a world without us, already a pond,
a cat, an orchard stuck with swords of light—
but the heart needs no reason for the belovéd.

Home

~ Dana Goodyear

Those last days in Hollywood—
Where were we going? We didn't know—
the johns came at midnight
and flung their broken condoms
to the ground; the next day, someone
dumped a car seat at our hedge.
Growling made it worse, those few times
we tried to sleep, curling from the sound
of hunger coming through the bedroom wall.
The furnace burnt the underbrush;
electricity shocked the pool;
dry as hands, the poison leaves
of the poison tree flew from the roof,
where one night, years ago, while
we watched "Play Misty for Me,"
wind played the fence wires'
anguished vocal cords, a lowing
loud as a mourning cow.
This imperfect world.
We are going, we are almost gone.
An accident: your globe dashed,
blue fragments puzzling the floor,
a cosmic question on your face.

The Bird That Begins It

~ Jorie Graham

In the world-famous night which is already flinging away bits of dark but not
quite yet
there opens
a sound like a
rattle, then a slicing in which even the
blade is
audible, and then again, even though trailing the night-melt, suddenly, again, the
rattle. In the
night of the return of day, of next-on time, of
shape name field
with history flapping
all over it
invisible flags or wings or winds—(*victory* being exactly
what it says,
the end of night),
(it is not right to enter time it mutters as its tatters
come loose)—in the
return I

think *I*
am in this body—
I really only think it—this body lying here is
only my thought,
the flat solution
to the sensation/question
of
who is it that is listening, and who is it that is wanting still
to speak to you
out of the vast network
of blooded things,
a huge breath-held, candle-lit, whistling, planet-wide, still blood-flowing,
howling-silent, sentence-driven, last-bridge-pulled-up-behind city of
the human, the expense-
column of place in
place humming....To have
a body. A borderline
of ethics and reason. Here comes the first light in leaf-shaped coins.
They are still being flung at our feet. We could be Judas no
problem. Could be
the wishing-well. Right
here in my open

mouth. The light can toss its wish right down this spinal
cord,
can tumble in
and buy a wakened self....What is the job today my being
asks of
light. Please
tell me my job. It cannot be this headless incessant crossing
of threshold, it cannot be
more purchasing of more
good, it cannot be more sleeplessness—the necklaces of
minutes being tossed
over and over my
shoulders. The snake

goes further into the grass as

first light hits.
The clay
in the soil gleams where dew withdraws. Something we don't want
any more of
flourishes as never
before. I
feel the gravity
as I sit up

like a leaf growing from the stalk of the unknown
still lying there behind me where sleep just was. Daylight
                                                                      crackles on the sill. Preparation
                                                                      of day
                                                                      everywhere
                                                                      underfoot. Across
the sill, the hero unfolding in the new light, the
                                                                      girl who would
                                                                      not bear the
                                                                      god a
son, the mother who ate her own grown
                                                                      flesh, the god
                                                                      who in exchange
for Time gave as many of his children as need be
                                                                      to the
                                                                      abyss. It is
                                                                      day.
The human does not fit in it.

How to Prepare for an Emergency

~ Kelle Groom

A boy from another country said he would never get out without my
help, cleaning offices for a plane ticket, but I was as helpful as the
history of silverware. I saw bodies wrapped in plastic in snow after
he left, his father losing money, mother losing weight—it was like
another planet, a dinner table from the last few centuries. There will
be *no gasoline available, no power. You might be far from home. The
money in your pocket will have to last. You get the picture.* When disaster
strikes, you will be the one following. When you come across the
handwriting of one you loved, it will be everything you knew. Paint
yourself a turnpike, river green, and place a fingertip on your face,
disappear in algae, tiny flowers. The time to prepare is gone, carry
a pair of walking shoes, compose six square feet, take note of a few
traumatic moments, waste paper. Don't count on being able to make
it back.

[KIMIKO'S CLIPPING MORGUE: **BRAIN** FILE]

~ Kimiko Hahn

BRAIN: "In Pursuit of a Mind Map, Slice by Slice"

BRAIN behavior: see SHAME, DISTRUST, OCD/neurotransmitters, Rapunzel syndrome, etc.

BRAIN misc.: "Flame First, Think Later: New Clues to E-Mail Misbehavior"; sealed manila envelope labeled *correspondence, her vitals*

BRAIN memory: "Memory Implant Gives Rats Sharper Recollection"; "No Memory, but He Filled In the Blanks"; "Researchers Create Artificial Memories in the Brain of a Fruitfly," photo of Rei tottering on sandy path as Miya runs toward me, the camera—scribbled on back, girls' first summer on Fire Island

BRAIN PAN: [empty]

BRAIN DRAIN: [empty]

BRAIN and head syn.: attic, bean, belfry, brain box, conk, dome, noddle, noodle, grey matter

BRAIN dreams (see DREAM THEORY)

BAIN [sic], *origin Old English* bana, *thing causing poison (see DUPLICITY)*

[file without label]: *Spirit Photograph Exhibit/admit two,* lavender lace thong, two flattened Chinese handcuffs

BRAIN fever: .... 2. a medical condition where a part of the brain becomes inflamed and causes symptoms that present as fever. The terminology is dated, and is encountered most often in Victorian

literature, where it typically describes an illness brought about by a severe emotional upset.

BRAIN poetry: Blake, "Mad Song"; Dickinson, "I felt a Funeral, in my Brain"; Poe, "The Haunted Palace"; Jeffers, "Apology for Bad Dreams"; Anne Sexton, "Angel of Flight and Sleigh Bells";

BRAIN Shakespeare: " these paper bullets of the brain," "In this distracted globe," "dagger of the mind," "Raze out the written troubles of the brain," "Memory, the warder of the brain."

BRAIN split (see CONSCIOUSNESS, see WIFE)

EVEN A THERAPY DOG COULDN'T GET THE VETERAN OUT OF HIS SRO TO PICK UP COFFEE AT THE 7-11

- Kimiko Hahn

the earth opened up — a voracious maw 325 feet across and hundreds of feet deep, swallowing 100-foot trees, guzzling water from adjacent swamps and belching methane from a thousand feet or more beneath the surface.

Biopsy

- Kimiko Hahn

... about 25 acres and still growing, almost as big as 20 football fields, lazily biting off chunks of forest and creeping hungrily toward an earthen berm built to contain its oily waters. It has its own Facebook page ...

Genocide

~ Kimiko Hahn

It was nearly 16 months ago that Dennis P. Landry and his wife, Pat, on a leisurely cruise in their Starcraft pontoon boat, first noticed a froth of bubbles issuing from the depths of Bayou Corne, an idyllic, cypress-draped stream that meanders through swampy southern Louisiana. They figured it was a leaky gas pipeline. So did everyone else.

She Offered Her Neighbor's Husband a Bit of "Harmless Fun" at an Airport Motel

- Kimiko Hahn

The gas floated up; the rock slipped down. The result was a yawning, bubbling sinkhole.

Note

~ Kimiko Hahn

The italicized texts in "Even a Therapy Dog Couldn't Get the Veteran Out of His SRO to Pick Up Coffee at the 7-11," "Biopsy," "Genocide," and "She Offered Her Neighbor's Husband a Bit of "Harmless Fun" at an Airport Motel" are all from "Ground Gives Way, and a Louisiana Town Struggles to Find Its Footing" by Michael Wines, *New York Times*, Sept. 25, 2013.

Smells Like Every Grief I Meet

~ Jennifer Michael Hecht

I want your arms and bring your legs.
It's good to lose along with friends.
Over-the-wall was once more heard,
But we all go down in a dirty word.

Hello, hello, hello, how low?
I measure every grief I meet
with narrow probing eyes.
I wonder if it weighs like mine
Or has an easier size.
I'm the featured creature, fetch the bleach.

Hello how low?
There's grief of want, it's more dangerous,
and grief of cold, which does nothing but restrain us,
a sort they call "despair;"
I found it hard, it's hard to find.
I feel cryptic and contagious,
I'm in anguish, entertain us.

Enlightened to a larger pain and state of mind.
The grieved are many I am told.
Through centuries of nerve.
And what could bring solace?

I measure every grief I meet
and though I may not guess the truth
A piercing comfort it affords
To act the sleuth and know that some
are like my own
Hello, hello, hello, how low?

When it's dark out, it's less dangerous,
It feels sorry and disclaims us.
Here we are now, entertain us.

I measure every grief I meet
with penetrative arts.
I wonder if it acts like me
or hives in buzzing parts
and hides its ugly parts.

O. Poetry. I want to trust
and thus presume.
I want hope
in a hat
to fly in
on her broom.

It's hard not to feel like a failure
when you're lonely amid seven billion.
Starts to look like the problem is you.

In the Great Depression
everyone lost everything and everyone
blamed himself. You can see it in the
photographs that won't look back.
So it is my turn to not want to look
at the camera. So I try. I'm wrong
not lazy, not defiant, quiet.
I don't know who thinks I'm crazy.

Untitled

~ Bob Hicok

I had a vasectomy — held the chunk of vas deferens —
spaghetti, I told the doctor — nibbled it — al dente —
he called me insane — I called him a Republican
& reminded him of property rights — that it
was mine — that I could wonder what barrenness
tastes like and fulfill my intellectual destiny
if I wanted — though men aren't
barren — women are
lovely — my wife is sleeping and — awake and
beautiful — she kissed the scar — kissed the reason
for the scar — and where I planted the inch
of me — nothing grows — unless rain
waters dirt — then mud flowers
from me — then I see myself
at seventy and — eighty and
staring at the door — at these children
of soil — these ghosts
of my sperm — coming to see
if we're ok — vasectomy
because I worried — because I couldn't answer
this question — if a baby
cried — if a baby cried
for hours — if I had
fists — a hammer — would that baby
cry long enough to become a man
I put a cross on the booth
where our relationship died.
I got the idea for the cross
from the highway, which resembles
a graveyard at the curve
where fog lives. White booties
dangle from one, the name Daniel

scrawled as if an earthquake
were grieving. One of us
wanted children and one of us
wanted to be a child, I forget
how much I had to drink
to forget how that went.
But I never drove angry
or drunk, at least I wouldn't
call it driving.

NO WHERE

~ David Huddle

"Hopper's people have no where to go…"
—Tony Magistrale

Lately I've begun mourning its absence,
that beloved *Where* that made our lives
so incorrigible, every morning sun so
dependable, kept us from doubting the truth

of spring lilacs. *Where* had trees, grass, a brook
that used sunlight to make rocks pretend to be
diamonds. *Where's* blue dome was where God hid
shyly and let third graders cherish the fragrance

of their spelling books. Oh, ever-morose Hopper—
I know it's not your fault. You just discovered
those people, they were already Republican deep
in their bones, already planning to hijack *Where*,

haul it off to their grim castles, lock it up
far back in the old slave quarters, guarded
and safe, out of sight of the ten million fools
who irresponsibly loved such dearest distance.

Two Martinis

- Andrew Hudgins

Into the underdome of a blue umbrella,
more than just a little drunk, two
martinis tilted uphill into evening rain
decreasingly askew.

The Past Is an Accident Made of Glass

- Andrew Hudgins

Faceted flakes of glass, like minute
arrowhead chippings from a battlefield
or hunting ground, work through my skin,
as if squeezed up by frost heaves
on a prairie now cut into eroded furrows.

Fewer and fewer emerge as the wreck
recedes into memory, a slight tenderness
as another surfaces, sometimes pain,
and sometimes I simply wake and find
history's blood glyphs on my pillowcase.

THE DECLINE EFFECT

- T.R. Hummer

She went on four legs at morning into the Marketplace
   of the Virgins. She bought potatoes and an onion
And the tail of an ox for soup. The fountains of the forum
   healed every supplicant. She watched a crippled girl
Strap on marble legs, and a foaming politician
   cough up a herd of swine. All shadows shrank.
She stood straighter as the archbishop untied her tunic.
   At noon they talked over glasses of grappa and The Holy
Father described to her the mechanism of the erosion of truth
   in the inner sanctum. Outside, twilight arrived
Like an epilogue. She waited in the proscenium, tail forgotten,
   for the last bus to her distant neighborhood, depending
On her cane to support her there in her well-earned habit.

Elephants

~ Mark Irwin

Within their wrinkled tents you can hide a city's cares: Grey

breathing buildings that move through fog— or in sunlight

the dusty columns of legs. On TV I saw a man in Pakistan beat one

into submission. Next day it became a mountain whose snow would not stop falling.

Breathing, smelling, touching, the trunk like something divine come down,

and the trumpeting's ravenous and holy wail, still echoing through Asia & Africa, while infinite are a savannah's creases around the eye. The imponderable

weight of each body, and of hands still forming one from the thick mud of paper mâché.

Into Light, Into Another Day

~ Judy Jordan

Even before the snow, the design was nebulous:
hollow steel hooped to four-by-fours and studs
and repairs the chaos of a high school gym's discarded
shower curtain strung aft to aft and rope-rigged to the steel
just where it wrested itself from the warp and bend
and break from the weight of back-to-back wet winter snows.

Floundering ship that never keeps out water or leaves its moorings.

Each gust of wind rips the greenhouse plastic
from the frame, shaking the bedding shelves,
then slams it back down so that I grow to believe
this tattered plastic is the loose skin that separates
the worlds and I feel expectant, self-conscious,
aware of an unknown gaze, waiting for something,
perhaps death, that voice which will come to me,
reach into my salted being and jerk that unknown part
of me through my mouth's roof to blasted air and the smell

of burnt rubber. But now I know only the frog's moans
from underneath the bed, the lightning-felled tree
sending out fresh stems all along its trunk, the green
furl of new plants, the tender, moist
stem and that smell, unnamable and new,
something clean, reborn, stretched from somewhere,
some strange and waiting place, to here.

A simple enough idea, the half of the greenhouse
with the huge gas heater collapsed, so
where do you go but to the other half: the cot

I sleep on, rising every two hours to chunk wood
into the brick-lined fifty-gallon drum, the annuals
and perennials leaf-dark from cold, shifting a little
when the warm air sifts and fingers
through the tangle of bedding flats.

East on the Interstate away from the University town,
then exit and exit again past the estates
and horse farms and old TV sitcom stars mapping
Keswick like some hot, blue-starred galaxy and finally
this two mile, dead-end dirt and gravel, this greenhouse
and the two thousand acres of paper-company land that swallows it.

The plate, the spoon and knife, the cast-iron pan,
rope I pull myself up with, futon,
pillow, seams bleeding feathers,
desk lamp hanging by its cord from the metal hoops
beside the one pair of dress pants, the sun-splotched coat,
water hose coiled on the ice-slivered gravel,
how I name myself now. And this:

> flats of plants, flats of bone-flecked wet, black loam,
> slim seeds slipped into soil so rich it breathes.

Through plastic, the winter sun looks like polished stone
and all of outside washed in a strange yellow light,
the roof of clouds unbroken and full of rain.
I work all morning, elbow deep in sphagnum and peat moss,

StoneheadBigBeefSnowCrown
PrimeroNapoletanoMarjoramSweet
TequilaSunriseValenciaMortgageLifter

Skies crosshatched in cold drizzle, sun gauze-wrapped
as the ground rises, returning from the snow stone by stone,
wind filled with the wing beats of crows.

TurkishOrangeRosaBiancaDiamond
DixieGoldenQuadratod'AstiRossi
TennesseeCheeseBloodyButcherBoxcarWillie

If clouds are the clothes of gods hung out to air,
then today it's the lesser gods whose rags bunch
and tangle along the lines of heaven's alleys,
tied window to soot-grimed window.

SweetMillionCaroRichSiamQueen
BigBoyLemonBoyBetterBoy
JetsetterMuchoNachoFinoVerde

On days like this my body unhinges: this focus on particularities,
this disappearance into pain, teaching me what death is,
tumbling out of myself as I lay another seed flat along
the wood shelves gray with age then pull myself up,
though sometimes the baseball-bat beating of pain is so great,
I think surely someone else tugs me into light, into another day.

BigBerthaEarlyGirlSweetBabyGirl
BrandywineCaspianPinkCelebrity
LavandulaAngustifoliaNepetaCataria

Stretched out now, seeds sipping soil and water,
transplants' bruised roots tender and dependent
as infants incubating under this artificial sky

and as I throw more wood on the fire,
raise and lower the pump's handle, turn the hose
to the finest mist, outside rain begins to fall, earnest
and steady, to the snow-saturated earth, tunneling
through mud and roots and burrows of shivering
mice and falling on raptors scouring the fields
for those mice, on worm and cardinal and starling,
on ratsbane and rats alike, rain to rise again, surely as the dead
on their last walk, their trek across the trail of stars
we call the milky way, soon to rise again, rise to air,

stumbling along as all things must, on this light-dazzled,
star-spangled bridge of terror we say yes to,
this thing we call life, lucky, lucky, labyrinth of life.

07.29.09. Bourg d'Oueil

~ Pierre Joris

to learn the shadow
shapes of the birds
of prey in a late

sky — while the coals
in the kanoun turn
from black to white

having glowed through
a blood-like red
— and flies drink this ink.

Sour Birth

- Pierre Joris

dear Anselm,

there may be a typo
in that poem:
   the line "Just a sour birth"
should read
"Just as our birth"

unless the poem wanted it to be
the other way around.

Like a Steeple and a Flag

- Katia Kapovich

The last one, clean in a threadbare spiderweb,
the corpse of a moth, a needle in my brain.
Then the fall came and two beggars on one curb
fought: the spin of poverty had somehow
brought them together
on one of those mornings, otherwise peaceful and
droning on like a Muslim prayer.
Then they embraced each other like a flag and a steeple.
A fraternal kiss or last meeting of the eyes
would hardly have been appropriate
under the circumstances.

People got questioned by police
that arrived on the scene and wanted to "have a word"
(what kind of word? I thought) with the witness,
me. I just scratched my head.
"What a beautiful death!" as Napoleon in *War and Peace*,
not me, said that to his generals during a pause
on the battlefield next to a body lying flat.
One must have generals around to say something like that.

Doctor Knows the Blues
- Marilyn Kallet

There are worse things than fried pie, Lou says.
Like what?
Like fried Ding Dongs, fried Moon Pies.

Last night at the Bijou Lou urged me to say hello
to Barry, the mandolin player,
throwback to forty years ago.

I was, as my mother would have said, "shacking up"
with Barry's roommate, the lead singer.
We were screamers.

I'm sure that's what Mr.
Mandolin remembers.
How we kept the boys up.

They wanted to be us.
We wanted to be us,
until we didn't.

"Don't do anything
you don't want the whole world
to know about!" my mother used to say.

Too late, Ma.
Let the Circle Be
Unbroken, forty years

down the line, or smash it
to bits
when the band

plays Dorsey's "Doctor Gonna Fix It,"
and I try to beg off, "We were not friends,
Mr. Mandolin and I."

Lou insists, "But you were there!"
There are worse things
than fried pie.

I can't speak of them, even now,
not to Lou. Not to the poem.
Little deaths. Then real ones.

Aegis in Abstentia

~ Christopher Kennedy

All the particulars have formed, all the accumulating carbon atoms that sought each other out in the wake of exploding stars to create what is human, now solidly headed toward the origins of decay. All of it leading to this moment, my hands surrounding a cup of hot coffee in the fifties luncheonette, oldies spinning on the speckled blue jukebox, and the realization of flesh, fading toward fragile bone, like the blood rush of the spacewalk astronaut become untethered, the irrevocable moment that begs forgiveness that cannot be attained.

I ask the ether for a spoon, pour sugar from the glass dispenser on to the black Formica and try and try to read the signs, the constellations the granules form, my own night sky. The waitress, eyeing the mess I've made, seems less and less intrigued by my musings, and I'm loath to explain to her again the seriousness of my mission, the importance of which to her must seem just another random spill.

Six Blessings and A Curse

~ Richard Kenney

Plans

Weigh odds. Pray. Pay bills.

Tell truth. Love well. Serve real gods.

Meanwhile, daffodils.

And That?

Cut forest? A moor.

Drained swamp? A field. Extinct sea?

That's a prairie. Love?

Fashionable

What world wants, world eats.

Or, like a vast pregnancy

Sometimes, what it needs.

Rock

Dear us, united

In pluck. Pluck plus black luck. Pluck

Deracinated.

Hard Place

Should you feel failure?

You're not at the best vantage.

Touch wood. Splinters. Braille.

Orrery

Lo! Lord's swung bola

Circle and parabola–

Love, too, oo-la-la.

To the Cobbler Who Put the Squeak in My Boot

~ Richard Kenney

May you bruit

about churches, crunching croutons,

in starched armor. May your plate suit's

squeak match mice (your pendant earrings)

well within hearing

of a squadron of peering

finger-wagging, very unhappily

lip-shushing hypercontrarian

librarians.

May you marry one.

May you honeymoon sunning

in traffic, in a cab whose ignition key is ever turning,

while its engine is ever running

'Did He who made the lamb make thee?'
~ John Kinsella

More on 'all fours' than upright,
two cousins in dry dirt by wire fence,
a lamb either side of the bent gate.
Head down tail up, the lamb
on the cousins' side is working
gaps, sniffing and tasting spaces
between posts, tail intact, still
to fall off. Each becoming alike.

The search for green is aberrant
as new world order outside mothers'
orbits. Pining for feed. Snippets
of straw glisten on dirt quiet
with grain, ready to sprout
when rains come. Green
will be short, and conversation
before words fully form, lambent.

All are lexical.
Eyes yearn and speak.
Even silence is verbal,
insisting we remember.

If You Were John Riley

- David Kirby

This didn't happen to you, but it would have if your name
were John Riley and you had joined the army in 1845
with thousands of other Irishmen who couldn't land
any other job but then found yourself fighting your co-religionists
in Mexico even as you were being starved and beaten

by Protestant officers who called you "hairy ape," "Papist,"
"Paddy." So off you go with several hundred equally
disillusioned sons of the Green Isle to form the Batallón
de San Patricio and fight on the Mexican side. And since
you've come this far with me, reader, let me ask you

two questions: (1) Is that a good story or what, which isn't
really a question, and (2) Is truth stranger than fiction?
Answer: It depends on the fiction. Balzac, Flaubert?
Not so strange; pretty workaday, pretty routine.
But Dumas and Dickens? Those are the fellows to go

to for your big bow-wow moments, your sudden intakes
of breath, your hey-wait-a-minutes, not to mention
your there-but-for-the-grace-of-Gods. Or take *Pygmalion*,
where Professor Higgins, who is going to India to meet
Colonel Pickering, runs into Pickering in Covent Garden,

the colonel having come to London to meet him.
Or Jean Anouilh's *Eurydice*, in which the lovers see each
other for the first time in a train station; had a child cried
or a bird flown overhead, one or both might have
glanced away, and there'd be no story. Fair enough,

but isn't the real-life encounter between Mick Jagger
and Keith Richards more delicious than anything
a pair of playwrights might have dreamed up? It's 1960,
and the two teenagers meet at Dartford Station,
and Mick is carrying albums by Chuck Berry and Muddy

Waters, and Keith says, Oh, you dig those cats, too,
huh? and they board the same train to London,
the Rolling Stones are born, and music is changed
forever. Years later, another band, Dire Straits, would
sing, "Everybody's looking for / Somebody's arms

to fall into." Ha, ha! They didn't mean Mick and Keith,
but they might as well have, since those two cuddled
like kittens when the going was good and fell to
clawing and spitting at each other when the going
got even better and are still together after fifty years,

like many another grumpy old married couple.
In 1847, the St. Patrick's Brigade was defeated
by their former comrades in arms, and John Riley,
along with six others, was stripped to the waist
and given fifty blows with a rawhide lash—fifty-nine

for Riley when the officer in charge lost count.
Then each was branded on the cheek with a "D"
for "deserter," though Riley's D was upside down,
so they branded him the right way on the other cheek.
After the war, he returns to the Mexican army

as a colonel and then begins to slowly disappear
from history, though an American dragoon claims later
that Riley married a rich and beautiful Mexican woman
and raised a loving family. Is that possible? I know
you believe it, reader, whether it's true or not.

This poem's almost over, and you've come this far,
so you've already bought in the way people do when
they start reading something and follow it all the way
through to its conclusion, and while most of us postmodern
folk are a more than a little leary of the happy-ever-after

ending, you wouldn't want me to leave you with a raw
back and two branded cheeks, would you, so let's just
say you're moseying through a plaza in Hermosillo
or Nogales when suddenly you look up to see a woman
looking out over her balcony, and she sees you

and smiles, and here the poem's going to have to refer
to yet another fictional work because, if a writer
has already made your point better than you ever could,
then why not let him or her do the talking, and here
I'm thinking of, not Shaw or Anouilh or any of your other

top-shelf authors mentioned earlier, but the J. D. Salinger
whose story "A Girl I Knew" has a narrator who says
of the girl in the title, "she wasn't doing a thing
that I could see except standing there, leaning
on the balcony railing, holding the universe together."

POEMS

Karl Krolow

Karl Krolow: *Poems*, translated from the German by Stuart Friebert

KARL KROLOW, a gathering of whose poems are presented below, was by any measure a giant of twentieth-century German letters. He made his mark early and often, with poems, translations (from the Spanish and French, chiefly; occasionally American), and criticism, later adding prose to his staggering output, which includes a number of Selected Poems (decade by decade), each with a life and mind of its own. Famously saying he didn't write just for readers, but also for "so-called dead objects, for landscapes, cities, gardens, street corners, animals, for the air, the light above a particular object, for the stone and its pores, for sadness, bodily pain …" the list goes on—reminding of Virginia Woolf's dictum that the writer must be able to distinguish the light from one day to another—Krolow ranged across many subjects and themes, in a panoply of voices, at once abstract and detached; but so focused and concentrated that what is observed becomes intimate, even voyeuristic at times, without failing to illuminate basic human wants, needs, and values. Fond of quoting Flaubert, Krolow seemed intent on eventually "writing a book about nothing," which at the same time would somehow be about every-thing.

When Krolow received the Büchner Prize in 1956, the highest literary honor in West Germany, his remarks, unlike Celan's, for instance, did not refer even in passing to his life during the Nazi period—a near occasion of sin, or worse, as some current critics complain. A close reading of his work, however, will give the reader some sense of Krolow's way into, if not back out of, the penumbra of those frighful, frightening years. The "record" also confirms that, perhaps to atone for personal failures for remaining in Germany while other writers chose exile or fled for their lives, Krolow was often generous to a fault regarding the work of others, especially of Jewish writers; and he helped turned the tide of dismissal to appreciation, notably championing the work of Celan and Nelly Sachs. As a critic, a judge of major literary competitions, he spent much of his life taking account of what his contemporaries were up to. Few writers who lived during Krolow's time were without his direct or indirect support. (Thanks to Suhrkamp Verlag/Berlin for permission to print the Krolow poems.)

Goods and Chattels

Someone's laid
leaves on our eyes.

Cool, the green.
It smells of beetles
and crickets. A kiss
quickly arrives
out of the air.

Spring's
a mechanical nightingale.
Stuffed birds
hover more intimately
on the wall.

No reason
but out of the water's silver
a gold coin:
how the moon rises.

The goods and chattels of love
are quickly spent.

Siebensachen

Jemand hat uns
Blätter auf die Augen gelegt.

Kühl ist das Grün.
Es riecht nach Käfern
und Grillen. Ein Kuß
kommt schnell hinzu
aus der Luft.

Der Frühling
ist eine mechanische Nachtigall.
Ausgestopfte Vögel
schweben inniger
an der Wand.

Ohne Grund
wird aus Wassersilber
eine Goldmünze:
so geht der Mond auf.

Die Siebensachen der Liebe
sind rasch vertan.

(1965)

Abyss of the Minutes

While you're making words during,
they've got the better of it
at this moment: –
we go down together.
Who's screaming? I'm keeping
someone's mouth shut. Love's noises
are always too loud.
Drowning or choking to death –
one hand goes around the other's throat.
It's hard to keep from squeezing.

While you're making words during,
they've got the best of it.
They're greedy and answer hoarsely.
Angels and agreeable animals,
steaming in the hot bath,
disappear under the little finger,
which consumes and is consumption.
Scream – more, more! – they'd like
to be torn to pieces, and
when you make words,
they've got the better of it.
Beds like snakepits.
They don't feel any pain.
They want everyone to watch:
that makes them still wilder.
Hydrophobia bites in, and the skin's
rolled up, tastes of salt,
blood and what
comes out of bodies.

Bang on: I'm happy.
The words, the words. We plunge
all tangled up like a skein
into the abyss of the minutes.
You're insanely good all right.
Abuse me. I'm dying.

Minuten-Abgrund

Wenn du dabei Worte machst,
haben sie mehr davon
in diesem Augenblick: –
man geht gemeinsam unter.
Wer schreit? Ich halte jemandem
den Mund zu. Immer zu laut
sind die Liebesspektakel.
Ertrinken oder ersticken –
die Hand legt sich um die andere Kehle.
Es fällt schwer, nicht zuzudrücken.

Wenn du dabei Worte machst,
haben sie mehr davon.
Gierig sind sie und antworten heiser.
Engel und gefällige Tiere,
dampfend im heißen Bad,
vergehen sie unter dem kleinen Finger,
der genießt und Genuß ist.
Geschrei – mehr, mehr! – sie möchten
zerrissen werden, und
wenn du Worte machst,
haben sie mehr davon.
Betten wie Schlangengruben.
Sie fühlen keine Schmerzen.
Sie wollen, daß jeder zusieht:
das macht sie noch toller.
Tollwut beißt zu, und die Haut ist
aufgerollt, schmeckt nach Salz,
Blut, und nach dem,
was aus Körpern kommt.

Schlag zu: ich bin glücklich.
Die Worte, die Worte. Wir stürzen
zusammen als Knäuel
in den Minuten-Abgrund.
Du bist wahnsinnig gut.
Beschimpf mich. Ich sterbe.

(1997)

Fragmentary Day

Fragmentary day. Something's
not right.
People have been sitting at the table
too long, heartily laughing or
looking at one another suddenly.
Under the skin we're all
flesh and blood.
Everything's a matter of luck.
Someone cut his finger
opening a bottle of Mosel,
drank hastily, as if in a hurry.
No one can make himself safe
because it's getting too hot.
The hours breathed away pass
indifferently in the fierce green.
How long will time keep us together?
How long can one bear it?

Fragmentarischer Tag

Fragmentarischer Tag. Etwas
ist nicht in Ordnung.
Man sitzt zu lange bei Tisch,
lacht von Herzen oder blickt
sich plötzlich nur an.
Unter der Haut sind wir alle
Fleisch und Blut.
Alles ist Glückssache.
Jemand zerschnitt sich den Finger
beim Öffnen einer Flasche Mosel,
trank hastig, als hätte er es eilig.
Keiner bringt sich in Sicherheit,
weil es zu heiß wird.
Die ausgeatmeten Stunden vergehn
gleichmütig im heftigen Grün.
Wie lange hält die Zeit uns zusammen?
Wie lange hält man das aus?

(1975)

Puzzle-Poem

PERTINAX – not from the comics,
a Roman emperor,
before or after Septimius Severus.
We think of this and that.
Of Gaul
or a detergent,
as secretly exciting as
advertising for a stimulant.
Perhaps a plant of the same
name bloomed, which Linneaus
could no longer name.
Hunches deceive, but we suspect
the unusual.
I can't recall
someone in France
naming his dog that way.
For an aphrodisiac
there's something missing
it really depends on.
I'm at a loss, look in the lexicon.
A poor imagination won't cut it.
He really did exist.
Just get to the
right reference book.

Vexier-Gedicht

PERTINAX – nicht aus dem Comic,
ein römischer Kaiser
vor oder nach Septimius Severus.
Man denkt an Verschiedenes.
An Gallien
oder an ein Waschmittel,
auch geheimnisvoll anregend wie
Werbung für ein Stimulans.
Vielleicht blühte eine Pflanze
gleichen Namens, die Linnè
nicht mehr benennen konnte.
Ahnungen trügen, aber man ahnt
das Besondere.
Ich erinnere mich nicht,
daß in Frankreich jemand
seinen Hund so reif.
Für ein Aphrodisiakum
fehlt es an etwas,
auf das es ankommt.
Ich bin ratlos, schlage im Lexikon nach.
Schlechte Phantasie reicht nicht aus.
Es gab ihn wirklich.
Sieh du nur zu
im richtigen Nachschlagewerk.

(1983)

On the Run

The match fell apart
Someone drew to his face.
He fled. Yet he allowed
As how at least his toes and fingers
Grew through the wall,
Which separated him from others.
Everyone could add to
The image in the mortar
That they made of him.

And so, a wild boar appeared sometimes,
Which a strange insect
Or a bird was following.
The shapes changed, in which
He showed up on the wall.
Nights his whispers
Lay on the glass of neighboring windows.
From a distance he watched the effect
On the dreams of girls.

But no one will notice
anything but the tracks
of several of his limbs anymore
In the vertical white of the limestone.
By and by they'll disappear...

Auf der Flucht

Das Streichholz zerfiel,
Das man seinem Gesicht näherte.
Er floh. Doch ließ er zu,
Daß wenigstens Zehen und Finger
Durch die Wand wuchsen.
Die ihn von anderen trennte.
Jeder durfte im Mörtel
Das Bild ergänzen,
Das er sich von ihm machte.

So erschien manchmal ein Eber,
Dem ein fremdes Insekt
Oder ein Vogel folgten.
Die Gestalten wechselten, in denen
Er sich auf der Mauer zeigte.
Nachts lag sein Flüstern
Auf dem Glas benachbarter Fenster.
Von fern beobachtete er die Wirkung
Auf die Träume der Mädchen.

Aber von ihm wird niemand mehr
Gewahren als die Spuren
Einzelner Glieder
Im lotrechten Weiß des Kalks.
Nach und nach verschwinden sie...

(1956)

Sleeping

I'll tell this
later as a dream,
how I lie here hand and foot
my mouth slightly open
and lost in a region
without meaning and air,
totally dead, but easily
satisfied with really pretty
pictures, which mean nothing,
surfaces of color without background
and god-given qualities,
just gradations of some colors,
which change and were only
there whenever they
disappear again, and I slowly
sense a handkerchief on my eyes,
my faced turned
to the side.

Schlafen

Ich werde das später
als Traum ausgeben,
wie ich daliege mit Hand und Fuß
bei leicht geöffnetem Mund
und verschwunden bin in einer Gegend
ohne Sinn und Luft,
gründlich tot, aber leicht
zufriedengestellt von wirklich schönen
Bildern, die nichts bedeuten,
Farboberflächen ohne Hintergrund
und gottgegebene Eigenschaften,
nur Abstufungen einiger Farben,
die wechseln und die bloß
da waren, wenn sie wieder
verschwinden, und ich langsam
mit seitwärts gedrehtem Gesicht
ein Taschentuch auf den Augen
spüre.

(1970)

Pictures

Pictures get
along without syntax.
Freedom as a placard
has a fully-realized body,
which likes to view itself
and suppresses the truth
like all flags, which we
fasten to our hat while out
walking along in a
region, in which we think
we know our way around --:
life, which can bear a great
deal, but isn't true
if one holds it up to the light,
and pretends
as if it were completely distinguishable
from the illustrations of the sort named above.

Bilder

Bilder kommen
ohne Syntax aus.
Die Freiheit als Plakat
hat einen vollkommenen Körper,
der sich angenehm ansieht
und die Wahrheit unterschlägt
wie alle Fahnen, die man sich
an den Hut steckt unterwegs
beim Weiterkommen in einer
Gegend, in der man sich
auszukennen glaubt –:
Leben, das eine ganze Menge
aushält, aber nicht stimmt,
wenn man es gegen das Licht halt,
und das so tut,
als sei es vollkommen unterscheidbar
von Abbildungen oben genannter Art.

(1970)

World-Machine

Hour-glasses. Attributes
of the invisible world-machine,
slowly running and poetical
as an apparition --
one experiences the runoff
of history as something
falling through fingers,
while there's joyful shooting
at people, who
are no longer useful.
With pleasure the past
is worked up as the future.
The botany of dreams
wants to be learned,
in order to make use
of it for a utopia,
which won't be
stingy with atrocities.
The last card is never
misplayed. As soon as
tomorrow we'll know more.

WELTMASCHINE

Sanduhren, Attribute
der unsichtbaren Weltmaschine,
langsam laufend und poetisch
als Erscheinung –
man erfährt Ablauf
von Geschichte als etwas.
das durch Finger fällt,
während fröhlich auf Leute
geschossen wird, die
nicht mehr verwendbar sind.
Mit Genuß wird Vergangenheit
verarbeitet als Zukunft.
Die Botanik der Träume
will gelernt sein,
um aus ihr Nutzen
zu ziehn für Utopie,
die mit Grausamkeit
nicht geizen soll.
Die letzte Karte ist nie
verspielt. Schon morgen
werden wir mehr wissen.

(1969)

Nothing More than Life

Nothing more. Nothing else
than a trifle like
interrupted handwriting
in a school-book more than
forty years ago.
No secret. The past.
So it was with this and that,
an overturned chair,
cold beds without smells,
eyes, which see into trees
and violence, hand-wringing,
head-shaking and frugal
feelings – you noble wild game,
nothing more than life,
which leaves one, patiently,
soon or now, right now,
too early some say, too late
they mean.
What's left -- these
thick trees from then,
painted on the green precipice,
where I've led myself around,
the other bodies, their familiar
eyes turned toward me.
It's time to get ready.

Nichts weiter als Leben

Nichts mehr. Nichts weiter
als eine Kleinigkeit wie
unterbrochene Handschrift
im Schulheft von mehr als
vierzig Jahren.
Kein Geheimnis: Vergangheit.
So war das mit diesem und jenem,
ein umgeworfener Stuhl,
kalte Betten ohne Geruch,
Augen, die in Bäume sehn
und auf Gewalttat, Händeringen,
Kopfschütteln und sparsames
Gefühl— du edles Wild,
nichts weiter als Leben,
das einen verläßt, geduldig,
bald oder jetzt, jetzt schon,
zu früh, sagen welche, zu spät,
meinen sie.
Zurück bleiben diese
dichten Bäume von damals,
am geünen Abhang gemalt,
wo ich umher mich leite,
die andern Körper, die bekannten,
auf mich gerichteten Augen.
Es ist Zeit, sich fertig zu machen.

(1970)

No Ideas

No ideas – useful objects instead,
with air of equal quality above.
For a long time now no more of Rilke's things
in the tobacco stillness, which
a smoker leaves behind in the room.
Hurry up – feeling for whatever
one can grasp with a hand:
a bottle of red wine, a foot
with its toes.
What's that burning now, fire?
It's not letting up.
With open eyes I get
what I need. Use and consumption.
Let all of that burn for you
and afterward leave what's left to the dark.

Keine Ideen

Keine Ideen – dafür Gebrauchsgegenstände,
mit ebenbürtiger Luft darüber.
Seit langem nicht mehr Rilkes Dinge
in der Tabakstille, die
ein Raucher im Zimmer zurückläßt.
Komm bald – Gefühl für das,
was man mit der Hand umfassen kann:
eine Rotweinflasche, einen Fuß
mit seinen Zehen.
Was brennt denn jetzt, Feuer?
Es läßt nicht nach.
Ich bekomme mit offenen Augen,
was ich brauche. Gebrauch und Verbrauch.
Laß das alles brennen für dich
und dem Dunkel danach das Übrige.

(1975)

All Night, Give or Take a Sloppy Hour

~ Lance Larsen

My neighbor's patio light burns like an ember, burns cleanly, never mind circadian rhythms and light pollution, burns like the all-seeing eye on every soiled dollar bill in his wallet, burns to keep his house and lavender Coupe de Ville once driven by Liberace safe from burglars and hoods and communists who sometimes parachute into your own backyard dammit, burns like the wedding album of his dear departed Betty, so slim and lacy and untouched back then, burns too like guilt because he couldn't save her misfiring heart in the produce aisle six years ago, burns at 100 watts purchased in bulk at Ace Hardware, burns like the teeth of my cat hunting hummingbirds in his tangled Eden, burns for the cul-de-sac's greater good, like a flaming umbrella warding off the apocalypse and glue-sniffing teenagers, come hell or high water or marauding cougars spotted in the foothills of late, burns too like the paranoia that keeps him from attending Sunday meetings because his Mormon bishop wants to marry him off to a church hag widow, burns too like the fireflies of his childhood in the Ohio, which he and his friends would catch and smear on their faces till they glowed like nuclear goblins, ah, the Wordsworthian oneness with nature back then, burns too like the fire in my veins for my beloved who has gone to bed already and refuses to sleep out on account of the sentinel brightness next door, burns without respite, thus preventing our house from nightmaring properly, let shadows, let more dark matter bombard me in our upstairs hall, burns like too much knowledge and not enough faith, more murk, less particle and wave, more chances to close my eyes to my neighbor's hallelujah blaze and taste night, that sweetest of leaven, flooding me from within.

Memo To Be Read In 2023

~ Sydney Lea

–for Robin

Dear Self,

If you can make it through the next ten years, then please
Look kindly back on me. It took some significant doing,
But I struggled to set you straight. The work was heavy, yes,
After my confrontation with that tail-gating punk, for instance,
Although I was well past sixty when we two went nose to nose
(Never mind that he was young and he wore that bloody headband,
The splotches of blood his own, or perhaps another's– who knows?);
After I'd jumped in his face, and the kid, his tires squealing,
Had roared away from the corner in front of the general store
Where I'd gotten out to meet him, and where folks of the town stood
gaping;
After nearly coming to blows there, against long odds, I resolved
To learn from such a moment, one of the many: nothing

But remorse attends such behavior, no matter its occurrence
May be "justified." I resolved, that is, to educate you
In forbearance like that young man's, if that's what it was–
forbearance.
Did the lesson take, I wonder? To feud with some cranky foe,
Like barking at one of your children when she got teary or balky,
In the end becomes a matter of two little brats in a huff
At one another. I hope you'll have lifted your eyes from such petty
Nonsense, turning instead to the hills and counting your blessings,
Even if you can no longer climb those hills as I can
Today, however slowly? My aim was to tell you something:
The world is full of wonder. How flawed and blind you remained,
Back when you were me. This world that I'm describing–

I hope it will have abided, even if you've passed on.
I'd like for example to know that it will exhibit to someone
These long and wondrous shadows made by late winter's sun
On the snow that covers our lawn, where juncos, rotund, well-
groomed,
Hop seed to seed to seed, all spilled from the feeder that swings
Overhead, where nervous pine siskins flutter and make a display
Of the shadow-like striations, gorgeous and sharp, on their wings.
But mostly I hope you may see that matchless woman still,
Who stands some distance away from those birds and clearly adores
Their look, and then through the window, she offers me magical
smiles,
Adoring ones too, which stuns me. Seeing her still, you're
commanded,
To haul those same eyes down from the hills and to make them dwell

On that wife, that particular blessing, the one you should value more
Than all the uncountable others that in this life you've been granted.

I Lift My Mother to the Commode
- Lyn Lifshin

almost too late tho
it's as close to the bed
as the tub to the
toilet lid I kept her
company on, handing
her soap and towels.
My mother, who could
climb Beacon Hill in
5-inch heels at 70,
can't lift herself with
out my arms, my hands,
always too cold she
shivers. "If I just was
not so lazy," she sighs
which translates, "tired,
weak." The hospital bed
could be Everest. Our
awkward dance to lift
her hopeless as prayers
for mercy, a reprieve
but I try to not show my
fear and now see her
tremble as the doorbell

rings. Verizon, to install
a private line she'll be
alive less than a week to
use. Still on the commode,
my stranded mother is
lifted by this smiling man
as if it was part of every

day's phone service,
gently as if carrying a
bride over the threshold
into a new life

The Other Life

- William Logan

I possessed a secret life: the seedy coastal town,
the shuttered colonial of twining hallways,
a wife with the flaring prettiness
of my mother, a smudge-mouthed child or two.
Awake, I never thought of that other life.
The two existed in mutual ignorance,
until one night the rough fields
and the volatile scent of my wife—my *wife*!—
with her Liz Taylor grin, her shock
of blonde hair, rose from the smell
of my real garden. Had I died in my sleep,
I might have woken to that new life,
ignorant of what I had lost,
if indeed anything had been lost—
like the phosphorescent wake
trailing a swimmer in the bay.
My secret left the faintest trace:
the Atlantic over the dunes,
the north flecked with the fall
that *is* fall. One day the dream was gone,
had been gone some months,
like a gas flame blown out.

Bathroom Mirror

- James Longenbach

Often, when dazzled by sunlight,
You cannot see the thing before your eyes.

This is an experience unknown to mirrors.
Turn on the lights, they suffer no distress.
What lies before them is perceived with greater clarity.

When your hand reaches for the soap,
The mirror reaches for the soap.
When you inspect
Your face, it broods.

Are you free from ambition?
Scared by the thought of death?
Are you any kinder than you used to be,
Any better looking?
Have you learned, like other people, how to have fun at a party?

A chocolate savarin,
Then little glasses of sauternes.
I'd left the table to pee.

Had you permitted it, earth,
I would have loved you
Like a little bird
That picks up crumbs.

Chacruna Traz Luz/Chacruna Brings Light
~ Mary Mackey

I still have that photo of you standing on the bank
of the Juruá   naked   your hair tangled
your lips pursed in surprise   or perhaps terror

On either side of you   wearing only penis gourds
two Kashinahua (or maybe Tarauacá) are blowing
hallucinogenic snuff up your nostrils
either through hollow puma bones
or the leg bones of some small bird   now extinct
whose feathers you have woven into the wreath
you wear as a crown

on the back of the photo you wrote:
Chacruna traz luz/Chacruna brings light
Huaira, Punga Amarillo, Capirona, Lopuna Blanca,
Challucahaki, Camu camu

the head spirits are starting to speak
my body is dissolving

and then   in an almost indecipherable scrawl:
get me out of here!

Bridge on Unnamed Branch of Big Goose Creek

- Maurice Manning

It was my chore then to clear away
the wet leaves and pine needles
from the big butternut log across
the gulley wash below the house
in the middle step of the hillside where
my grandmother lived. Each end of the log
was tucked into a stone cradle
and someone had taken an adze and dressed
the top to make it flat enough
for her to walk across without
a rail or a rope. Cold mornings
she crossed the log in her long, dark way
down to the road to meet my aunt
or, later, the Stivers man, who drove her
to the old tipple where she worked
recording the numbers in ledger books
as the coal came down in trucks and away
again by rail or other trucks.
The snow would not stay white for long;
the world was turning inside out
in 1974, and little
by little, a kind of slow forgetting
was happening and something I loved
that would never stop filling my heart
was slowly going away for good.
I've kicked the butt-end of that log
in my sleep to wake the snake stretched out
along it. Gollie was the name
she called my aunt—the Stivers man,
she called him Feller; and she called me

that boy critter—bess hit's heart,
she said, bess hit's heart, God love.
Oh, there were other bridges—one,
a swinging bridge on Little Goose
I saw with a rotten plank hung down
and flopping like the sole of a shoe
below the black cables the day
after a girl fell through and drowned.
Most of my life has happened since
that day and still I find it sad.
Yet still I see the butternut log
fetched over less treacherous water,
and still the breath of God comes back
from the time that isn't over yet.

Two Dreams

~ Campbell Mcgrath

1. Norway

Dream in which I am an old man named Willi—in a certain sense I am Willi but at the same time Willi is the protagonist of the film I am watching at one remove, through a karmic veil or an antique lens. Afflicted with Alzheimer's disease, Willi lives in a rough, frontier town, which seems to be in Alaska. It is achingly beautiful, steep hills with views of boats in coves, a sweeping bay with vistas of ice floes and moon-blue glaciers. I am trying to get back to the town of my youth, a much smaller place even than this one, a stone-hut settlement along a fjord, like one of the abandoned Viking camps in Greenland. I am too old. My memory flickers like shadows in a forest. Soon it will vanish, and with it my true self, and so I desire to return to my roots and die peacefully, in a roofless cottage, surrounded by high cliffs, grassy meadows, black water, a pale blue northern sky. But first I want a cup of coffee, and fate conspires to keep me from having it. The coffee pot at the restaurant breaks. At the general store they say they are making some but it never arrives. Then I'm in a cargo van, leaving town, a narrow road snaking to the top of a hill through an orchard of pollarded trees, a vertiginous view over the craggy interior plains, wait, this is the wrong direction! I shout until they let me off and then, walking downhill through the orchard, I come to an old farmhouse, where a young widow lives alone. I see her inside, busily sweeping the floor. She is friendly and talks with me, though I am an old vagrant, and she refuses my help with her chores, happily accepting her difficult lot. She is a papermaker, smashing tree bark with stones by the stream, stringing the pulp into long sheets of coarse paper. Her hair is arranged in an unusual, frizzy corolla, which I know to be the old-fashioned local style, a peasant mode warmly resurrected in these modern times. She reminds me of a girl I went to school with, Tina, a girl I've known since kindergarten, whose mother was Norwegian—we are in Norway, of course! Tina now lives in Austin, Texas with an inoperable brain tumor, for which she travels to Houston to receive treatment, and two young sons she hopes to see into adulthood. To survive that long, to hold on, to endure. And then it is morning.

2. Brazil

In the dream he bites into a delicious fruit and finds that it is filled with seeds, black and gold, like small jewels. It is raining softly and there is a lizard on the windowsill and a kind of butterfly flitting among the leaves of the mango trees, pale green and orange, its wings like the veins of a leaf or sunburned skin beginning to peel. He sees the goats browsing on weeds, and he hears the hum of flies, the thud of green mangoes cracking the earth like taut paper. He is naked and as he watches in amazement his penis turns into a flower, skin breaking away like eggshell to reveal a smooth, green stem. His hair is no longer red, if it ever was. He is anxious, waiting for something important, for his wife to give birth at last, which she does, pushing forth two mottled eggs the size of oranges, the color of butter and straw. The first egg hatches on Friday—the taste of fish and coconut still fresh—a perfectly formed infant that could fit in the palm of his hand. And it has wings! A tiny, immaculate infant who flies right out the window, hovers like a hummingbird, then disappears into the shadowy orchard, so many rows of trees beneath a sky bearing down with the weight of ocean water in which, incongruously, the cone of the volcano has begun to belch black smoke. Why won't the other egg hatch? He is sure that inside it lives an even smaller figure, an old man with a long white beard, a black wool cap and a knobbed walking stick. Bats are eating insects in the twilight and he feels suddenly bereft, at the point of tears, as he comes to understand that the man inside the egg is not his father but himself. He is green and sinewy, pure vine, rooted to the ground even as the house has changed to resemble a ferry terminal. Taller than any tree he can see across the island, across the bay to the city, across jungles and rivers and oceans, all the way around the world, his vision chasing the sun like a bullet, like a retriever fetching a fallen fruit to his table. When he bites into that fruit black and gold seeds spill into his palm, fifty seeds exactly, one for each year of his life.

Hideout

~ Sandra McPherson

On muddied feet, I found the menstrual hut, the birthing compound, out on the island just as rain's troupe mobbed my solitude. I followed swans in the distance. Entered and departed intimate lodges with sleeping platforms robed in skins. Warm, windowless, safeguarding heat to live. Winter without. I admired the brushwood uprights of the lunar lair, the east-west stick-woven walls rain nourished as if they'd be able to grow like vines. Here, a woman's private core pressured her as it welled. She felt soothed, comforted by the asylum allowing her to bleed, making *her kind* evadable. I don't (or wouldn't like to) believe it signified complete dismissal to Lenape women. Our personal storms accept the benefit of blood.

I was always in the boat
that floated out of me.

I will miss those driftings
and the two secret swans

purling current and calling it
the next someone's

flesh-to-be.

Sister

~ Vadim Mesyats, translated by Dana Golin

Screech of scissors mid-leap,
Shimmy of washed dishes,
wallpaper peeling away
from the musty walls;
and in her giant eyes
the mystery of eternal lust,
all the more lustrous
in the moon's sheen.

Outside the window, like silos,
monolith snow-banks,
hard-boiled bushels
of silvery grain,
but the wheels depart
into the dark sans cargo
and careen off the rails
at the end of the road.

Tamed fire
on an iron chain,
scared senseless
by the owner's crop
presses its copper underside
against an empty barrel,
reluctant to enter
the house of his dreams.

Relentless dripping
of the kitchen faucet,
the tense precision
of the clock on the wall…
Darned with careful cross stitching,

the gash of the heart
closes gradually,
bolted shut by the warmth.

My sister—young,
chill-warped shoulders wrapped in fur—
picks up wild blackberries
with her frigid mouth,
brings the globs to her lips,
as though tinting them with lip stain,
resting for an instant
on a myth's golden stoop.

A candle in front of her,
as if lit before an ancient icon,
illuminates uncomfortably
her chaste visage
of a holy young virgin,
yet a complete enigma…
Out in the hallway,
a lowly manservant sighs…

Young Love

~ Carol Moldaw

Always short a card, nostalgia
lays out its dog-eared deck
in a horseshoe spread, chooses
from the apex an iconic image:
her head in his lap, his hand
ruffling her hair, the two of them
dreamy midday, as if sleep
the greater part of consciousness.
Cigarettes balanced on the rim
of a wrought iron table dangle
ash; for years they live
in the aura of inevitability
they radiate, in love
with a tautological logic:
It was. It had to be. Hindsight,
with its stacked deck, knows
what happens next
and so no doubt do you—
but they themselves, they,
poor lambkins, were blindsided.

Evening

~ Cees Nooteboom, translated by David Colmer

in memory of Hugo Claus

The blue chair on the terrace, coffee, evening,
the euphorbia reaching for absent gods,
full of longing for the coast, everything
an alphabet of secret desires, the last
he sees before the gloom,

the mist in his head. He knows
the shapes of words will disappear,
only dregs in his cup,
the lines disconnected

that once were thoughts,
never again a word
of truth. Dismantled grammar,
blurred pictures without a bridge,

from the wind the sound
but no longer the name,
someone said it would be so
and death was on the table,

a slow servant, waiting
in the hall, smiling stupidly,
leafing through his newspaper
of senseless items.

He knows all this, the euphorbia,
the blue chair, the coffee on the terrace,
the day that folds around him slowly

and then swims off,
a gentle beast

with its prey.

At a Certain Point in a Marriage
~ Idra Novey

Say a man enters and a woman
leaves the room.
                    Say the man loves her

but never says this. Say the scent
after she exits is tender
as a felled tree.

Say the man can't tell what it is, thinks
empty porches,
                orchids, the unjoining

of clouds. Say the woman puts on
a heavier coat, takes in again
                            her own perfume.

Say it is like smelling the heat lost
through a window
                all winter.

Say the man follows her to the hall.
Say he lifts her wrist
                    to his mouth.

FAUST, 1972
~ Sharon Olds

This time, Faust was a nursing mother –
on one arm, a nine-month-old,
by one hand, a four-year-old, and in the
backpack a Ph.D., now un-take-
backable. She was walking down the steps,
on which, four years before, in the Strike,
the English Department Administrator
had stood with the bandage around her head,
bloody where the night-stick had hit her when they tried to fight
past her to her students. Nursing Faust
descended, now, beside the Alma
Mater, who was no longer wearing her
Shirley Hess lookalike
red-blotched headdress. And no spirit
came up to the milk-fat graduate
to tempt her — she just spoke, herself,
to the one she felt within her, the one
she thought of as Satan. *Give me my own*
poems, she said, *and I'll give you back*
all I have learned (forgetting she had learned
almost nothing), *and the poems don't have to be*
good — just my own, the work of an ordinary
woman. Then they went to Tom's, for pancakes –
the worn, vinyl booster seat
and the high-chair — and it was either Mary,
or Betty, who took care of them,
one on her feet all day, weighing maybe
300, one maybe 80 years old,
which was just the way things were, nothing
Faust would try to do anything about.
Pancakes for three, and bacon, and an extra
plate for the ego's voice, in my day called Satan.

Napoleonic Series, 1974

~ Dzvinia Orlowsky

A dozen black-inked prints of erections, ghost-fleshed and silhouetted, each phallus prominently displaying an admiral hat, too few to be called an army – their siege not *absolute* – just quietly present in bright sunlight. I could tell by the way Agnes, a mid-forties conceptual artist, stared at me, her intern, that she hoped her project would shock me all the way back to Ohio, to my split-level brick home abutting 10 acres of barren winter fields, 30 miles south of Cleveland. But I'd seen body transformed: Cynthia AlBritton's Plaster Casts, Jimi Hendrix's iconic hard-on, *Penis de Milo,* molded from and fireproofed with dental alginate. It was a kind of visual daring we lacked in our Midwest day-to-day, though two years later the Cuyahoga River caught fire. Assigned to a corner of her studio, slouched over expensive graph paper, I connected dot-to-dots of Agnes's 3-D model universe, listened to the wash of street noise come in through her window, careful not to disturb her deep mood. *This* was going to get her in the art history books. She could tell by how readily they took to paper, cockades relinquished, their would-be nameless fame in the signature bulk and roll. But it wasn't what you'd call boner-worthy like Hendrix's long fingers, kinky hair and black ultra suede plumed hat, purple scarf and silver loops, air-humping his *Wild Thing* Fender Strat, dropped to his knees, squirting lighter fluid over its Black Diamond strings, the world on fire.

The Freud Museum

~ Ruth Padel

Freud Museum, London, 2011

It's 1938. Here's moss on red brick
at Nutley Terrace and an old man displaced,
just not too late, by swastikas on the portico
in Vienna. His daughter has been caretaking
their flight. The trunks hold a red-topped desk,
T'ang camel, phials of Etruscan glass
dug up from tombs, a print of the Pharoahs
at Abu Simbel and a red-lozenge Persian rug.
All outward bound. *What is an object?*
Shards from a lost world, gone to ground
then brought to light. *And home?* A sleeping child.
A nick-of-time railway pass. A letting-go
of neighbourhood gone wild.
Breath on the mirror. A dog, a garden. Found.

Cosmology

~ Linda Pastan

Someone has spilled the moon
all over the trees;

someone is cutting down the trees,
branch by forked branch—

soon there will be nothing left
but kindling.

Why am I afraid of the dark
but more afraid of light, what it reveals:

this moonlight which lies everywhere
like a beautiful torn shroud;

the illumination of dreams, room
after room of dreams?

Is it the moon itself I fear,
in too many pieces now

to put back together? Or the stars,
light years away, my voice

traveling towards them
in a straight trajectory?

I fear the earth as it warms
and freezes; I fear your arms

which hold me a moment
then disappear.

For Night to Fall

~ Carl Phillips

You could tell from the start that the best
were frailing. We made the wishes we made,
beside the wishes we also hoped would
come true, for there's always a difference,
the way what we remember of what happened
is just memory, not history exactly, and
not the past, which *is* truth, but by then
who cared? The truth by then as a snowy
owl becoming steadily more indistinguishable
from the winter sand in twilight, feathered
emptiness filling/unfilling itself for no one,
no apparent reason – who? who says?
who says the dead are farther away from me
than you are? – across the hard, hard shore.

The Saw

- Anzhelina Polonskaya, translated by Andrew Wachtel

It's all over now. His saw's been sold.
Some hardworking guy bought it for a song
to cut down trees – birches and pines
and brush.
Five paper bills are lying on the windowsill.
Let's sit together for a moment.
Let's sit with our hands on our knees.
Life will go on, long and round as the earth.

No one. Never.

~ Anzhelina Polonskaya, translated by Andrew Wachtel

Don't wait for anyone, ever.
It's still getting dark. The blades of grass sharpen,
their outlines becoming invisible.

An empty road, What could be more timeless?

And if anyone should knock in the midnight darkness
here are twin keys that fit
any lock:
«No one.» «Never.»

People have a tendency not to return.

An Angel

~ Kevin Prufer

One morning,
a shoeless old man walked down his front steps
into the melting snow.

He couldn't remember where he'd left his car.
It wasn't under the carport,
it wasn't parked at the curb.

So he strolled down Prospect Avenue
toward the pharmacy parking lot
where he must have forgotten it,

though where the pharmacy was, he couldn't recall.
And what he meant to buy there eluded him, too,
and, anyway, he had forgotten his wallet,
and where was he going now?

His feet had been hurting him, but now they were numb,
now they felt all right, warm and strange—

And isn't it lovely how the flag
high above the used car lot
snaps in the spring wind?

The young soldier gave him a curious look,
but didn't say anything
so the old man kept walking

because he would be late for the service,
the enormous sun beyond the steeple,
filtering orangely through wet branches,

the glare of traffic lights and onrushing cars
confusing in the darkness,

and there are only two ways this story can end,
because the old man can't walk forever
and he is unlikely to grow wings.

Singer

~ Christina Pugh

If you've heard the cant of the auctioneer *(do I*
hear twenty-one), the voice of a tenor calling
among straw, don't you see how music
enthralls the marketplace? Singer, you
appeared to me alive again, clothed in
bright satin: I'd arrived at your party
in New York. In the clerestory, girls
were posing for a photograph, their skirts
sea-foam as my mother's was in 1956.
You closed your hand on mine so I could
see the ruined seam between our two
worlds, the living and the dead—neither
of us mothers. But if you live in my ear,
so I too might live again—as an inkling,
the flame between a number and the
welling of a wish that stops the cry:
So long lives this, and this gives life to thee.

Normalcy Bias

~ Lia Purpura

It's often not clear
if something wrong
is wrong at first.
At first you wonder
what *is* that, and
could it *be*? Not
that you want
to excuse it
exactly, but hope
something else
can explain it away.
Like friendliness.
Just horsing around.
On a city street,
where it didn't belong,
I once mistook
a small deer
for a very big dog—
the way years,
a lifetime
of good deeds
makes you think
something wrong
is unlikely.
Couldn't be. Is too awful.
Couldn't possibly live
so close to me.

Almost, But Never
~ Lawrence Raab

"This appealing legend," she explained
in the gallery while we studied the tapestry,
"does not correspond to historical facts."
I wanted to ask if knowing this changed
anything for her, or if my question,
which I didn't ask, was beside the point.

In the tapestry there were many oaks,
and many hunters on horseback among
these oaks, brandishing long spears as their dogs
raced gracefully beside them. And yet it appeared
nothing was moving. Was that the idea—
they were all helplessly trapped in the moment?

But she was recounting the legend,
most of which I'd missed. A heart was involved,
or a *hart*, or both, and a beautiful woman
tied to an oak, and two kings, each one
powerful and jealous. I wanted to ask
if this wasn't in fact very close to King Arthur,

but so what if it was, I didn't care, I just felt like
saying something so she'd have to look at me,
our tour guide, who was slim and lovely
and spoke with a light Italian accent, and who,
when pointing out some detail, almost, but never,
touched the surface of what we were trying to see.

Essay on No

- James Richardson

The pebble won't open its eyes, posing
roundly but softly its little
no to the light. Better

to be small and dark than concede
more than you should, and yes,
even the satin

yes of a violet is also
a petal by petal, point
by point *maybe*

or maybe not to the lazy
generalization of the air
that *It's all the same.* Shall we call

their reluctance *self*,
or maybe *form*? Vastness
and radiance alone won't cut it –

think of the terrible darkness
the sun is in – nothing
comes back to it, it can't, for all

its outbound *yesssss* of light,
see or listen (it's the moon,
isn't it,

we tell our troubles to?) *Yes* is
es- , to be. It is what is. God knows
there's more than enough

of that. Even he
feels he's said too much,
remembers fondly his first *No,*

let's wait and see, but now
there's no stopping
the expansion of his universe

from driving into the dark
though there may be
a hairpin turn, a fallen rock,

an oncoming universe
with no headlights, nothing to do
with its doubts

but drive faster. Heart knows
there's something about the best
offers that offers

to take itself back. My hand
is thankful for the firm
not mine (your hand) it is surprised

it knew was there, and all
the pleasure in these few
too many words is feeling them land

in the dark *not quite* behind your soft dark eyes.

Antelope

~ James Richardson

But language isn't about things, and nouns are the least of it. Probably the first word ever was inseparable from a gesture and a facial expression that went with it, something like *Hey!* When God showed Adam the first of the swift animals, he said *Ah!*, he said *Whoa!*

How the Sky is Made

~ Alberto Rios

We have camped out, eaten, filled ourselves,
Told the best stories we know,

And gotten tired. All of us sleepy,
We douse the fire, and watch as so much of it

Goes up, those sparks and bits and chuffs of smoke:
They suddenly make the sky, they suddenly

Go to their second jobs as stars in the night
And working as clouds in the horizon of the next day—

Fire, that ingredient for the making of the sky
We have forgotten.

Swerver

~ David Rivard

She was born for
the pleasures of swerving
and with a courage
as impractical as it was
necessary
beneath a harsh light bulb
in some Alberta hotel room,
not to play the fool
or push a hangman's cart.
She remembers
how summers there
had the excitable, slipshod languor
of strip poker,
but that winter snapped
like a brown rat trapped & frantic
in a wooden cage, a cage
she'd last seen flying through dark smoke,
her father having flipped it
with one furious hand onto a bonfire.
So it goes with
the impossible—
at 16 you think yourself
a connoisseur
of the inner-life for sure,
tho you're allowed
an occasional glimpse of the world
and how it looks
to others—10,000 colors
in the skin of an apple,
and not one of them red or green—
name one
and the future might

open for a moment in spite of all
your evil speculations.
She remembers how her mother
drowned the ticks in a mason jar
after they'd been pulled from
the garrison dogs,
the jar half-full of machine oil.
The first boy she kissed
spoke of superhumans & died later
of a brain hemorrhage.
She remembers all of this later. Later—
after much statecraft had taken place
and days that passed
like the sound of swan's wings in the fog
whenever she sat
by herself at a foreign picnic table.

INTERVIEW: PERFORMANCE ARTIST IN HELSINKI

~ J. Allyn Rosser

[***Translate this Page***]

How most for to explain what would I?
To appear against myself
always in separation
entailing backdrop by reintegration
as of the yellow and the lemon,
the paper and the tree,
like a prolongation of a part of living.

I only can mirror be that sound
from caves of their making.
Not mine!
But their thinking so *continues* it.
For is why I call out, one and one
and one and one, shards of a dark.
And if the hour is correct with me,
if I fail to drop a step,
they cannot abscond with their viewing
or unhook their hearts
in adjacency to such silence
as now begins: a far waiting
like ends of dreams of trains
not yet begun.
Like the disassembled drum.

The Subterrestial

~ Clare Rossini

I grew naturally
Barefoot

And what dust I shook from my feet   clouded the water in the tub
I climbed out   radiant

As the church's virgin-saint   looking to me
From the pedestal   of some perfect way   her stone eyes
        blind

To the predatory
Shadows retreating to the west

Where the last stand of oak   was sawed down, carted off   all the
        living
Branches still shuddering with leaves

And in their place, airy naves   of bungalows rising
The whine of the drills   a fraught jazz

The edge of my shovel   pierced the field's damp skin   the taste of
        clover
Bitter in my mouth as I   dug in, furious

As the day moon   whetted on a cumulus
The butterfly's trail   jigsawing above my head

The bungalows   growing walls   windows roughed in   my dimple
        of earth
Becoming cave

I slew sunlight   on my way down   groined myself   to a root
        tangle
(Don't tell me   a child is innocence

A child's the barbarian   buried beneath   the forum's polished floor)
Rain tat-tatting   on my sheet-metal roof   I withdrew

With the sly beetle   the radical worm
While on the hills around me   new doors fitted, oiled   swinging
        shut

Against the remonstrance
Of Midwestern clouds

Our House

~ Tomaž Šalamun, translated by Micael Thoms Taren and the author

In our house we have a tiger to warm our
slippers and a deer to open our cans.
The snow in front of our house is cleared by
a snail. In the woodshed near the lawnmower,
near the old map of Liverpool there are stars
drawn by chalk. In the morning spiders
are killed with clubs as they are only *le soir*
l'espoir and through the special metal cone
we shout how the boat has to be secured.
The man once in his life certainly sloshes,
the rabbits once in their life certainly
break their ear.

In our lands every popped balloon makes for
trauma as balloons are not restricted goods.
Fences are phenomenally rusty.
Palm trees bang on the wooden boxes and
the violinists have palm trees' body hair
between their shirts and sweater
sleeves. Globes are *Hochstaplers.*
Schmutzwelt anschauen Krech!

Sometimes someone rushes to Florence
and looks at David, but not really
We too have the Renaissance.
The melancholy **also** finances some special terms:
tschuketz, (always part of: *you are tschuketz*)
who will prepare the *becaccin* (always part of
sailing) and jump headfirst (into the sea).
In spring the clan undertakes the journey

to Triglav, so the worm of the decadence is
revealed, and who then coughs will surely soon die
and who will die will leave money to those who
are more resistent to the worm of
decadence.

One knows that Izidor Cankar perished from
the too-steep standard of his mind. Ther are constant
discussions about *mésalliances*, if they're good for
the blood or bad for the style. While walking on
Komarča someone shouts: Watch out! Watch out!
and to all foreigners we explain Savica
Falls for the sixty-seventh time.

On such occasions the author bites some
straw like *bezprizorni* in the times of NEP.
The destiny is where your ass is thrown down,
we all know it, therefore in our house we have
the tiger to warm our slippers and the deer
to open our cans.

The snow in front of our house
only God can clear.

Edna St. Vincent, M.F.A.

~ Mary Jo Salter

for Joseph and Carla Harrison

Chic and petite, blind to her destiny
of being hailed upon her death the worst
sometimes-excellent poet in history,
she ran the reading series, and ranked first
in her year despite some issues, namely those
pretentious, creaky sonnets emailed late
for workshop, densely wrought with "thee"s and "thou"s,
Apollo's "dewy cart," man's "frosty fate"…
Her classmates listened, bored, without a clue.
Still, they liked her, partly because she friended
everybody who asked, and fucked them too,
lending them each some notoriety
by blogging through the night how things had ended.
Plus, she knew people at A.W.P.

The House on East Eleventh Street

~ Grace Schulman

Sunset, winter. Light snuffed out. No twilight,
no second flare, as the woman leans,
rights herself again, and disappears

into the house, its whitewash chipped and peeling
but still ghost-white, boasting that it had shone
among brownstones. Now the house stays dark.

Once windows lighted up at dinners for twelve,
painters with new loves, sole with style.
On high walls, the year's bravura

in oils, in inks, spoke for the wholeness
of art above their makers' fractured lives.
A crystal chandelier shook with her kisses

and with her disregard – *not that disaster* –
flickering like her eyes when she unwrapped
a canvas, sized it up, followed each line,

and said, *It's like the Aztec carvings,*
the sun, the moon, the life, and suddenly
you're old. I call that painting back tonight

while watching hooded windows under a sky
starless and chilly. Soon she will sort
jottings which might either fill pages

or else be scattered in a breeze. A story's end,
perhaps. But wait. Sidling out of shadow,
a man in jeans with a wheeler bag swings open

the wrought iron gate, climbs broken steps,
stalls, presses the doorbell, lights go on.
New lover? Foreign guest? I don't know yet.

Cancel the ending. The story begins here.

Bechdel Test (TAKE TWO)

~ Maureen Seaton

M: Was there ever a time when you didn't want to be a poet?

D: By poet do you mean broad channel swimmer? Scarlet paper poppy painter? Collectible Lady Schick ballet razor? Dial-a-Girl (Scout Cookie)? Motherboard?

M: I wasn't even a little bored when I first discovered I could string words
across my chest and down my back.

D: You were.

M: There was.

D: Never a time when I didn't want to be blown away like a pilot light. Smashed before the start of the bash I brought my piñata to. Cryogenic when the globe spun tropical.

M: Queen of daft and deft, carnage and conception.

D: She who poetizes faithfully.

Breakfast at Starbucks with Egret

~ Martha Serpas

Don't think less of me, Reader.
In years to come, I am confident,
a footnote will be necessary.
But newspapers will still accompany
coffee, and poets will smoke
two-for-one cigarettes
over curled yellow pads
wherever the former are sold.

We saw, as we herded ourselves through the slot
of the drive-thru, a cattle egret
standing aside the mini-mike and menu,
noble and goofy as a stuffed giraffe.
Into the crotons it went
and snatched up a lizard in the straw
of its beak, belly-held it for a beat
before tossing it down
like popcorn. "Dinner for a week!"

my friend said to her frappé
just before the white-crested glutton swallowed
another appendage waving green.

Consider the egrets of the parking lot.

Consider you and me saying goodbye
over a two-pump mocha
and the plain dark roast that will suffice.

At the Cemetery

~ Alan Shapiro

Cloud cover from horizon to horizon
like an inverted topographical
map identical in scale
to what it models—

gray mountain ranges darkening
as they rise downward,
the crease of valleys
thinning upward

into paler grays, thinning and thickening
along lines that shift and merge
like a map in motion,
a phantasmal

time lapse of tectonic plates, of every
upsurge and subduction
going nowhere on
and on on

courses intricately fated, haphazardly
minute and massive while
below them sprays of
fresh-cut flowers

invisibly decay and leave
brief trails of sweetness
all along each newly
chiseled name.

Anesthesia

~ Jeff Skinner

Unasked return of faces
That once did but
No longer exist—black-haired
Nancy, Scott's bladed

Profile, Peter's beard, still
Shadow after shaving,
Amy (girl everyone loved)—
Rising through the Diazepam

The sense of the world
Must lie outside the world—
When I survived
Our accident I brushed by

My double going back—
O love, even ideas have eyes

Stop-Time

- Ron Slate

Frank McCabe bought on credit at my father's liquor store,
they had gone to school together. Finally my father said,
teach my son to play drums and we're even, for now.

Late afternoon lessons in his cellar, first the basics
rapped out on rubber pads, then rolls, drags, flams, paradiddles and
ratamacues.
Moving on to a real kit and the flair of fills, underbelly routines
of the bass and flights between cymbals, crash and sizzle.

While I practiced, he scribbled on charts for his quintet —
Thursdays at the Knotty Pine and weddings on weekends.
No lessons for most of the summer after his heart attack.

Autumn rain, water seeping up through linoleum tiles,
staining the peeling baseboards. Mold and mildew,
back beat and double time. Smoker's cough and drinker's nose.
Soon he set up his kit next to mine, laying out the opening bars
of "From This Moment On" and I'd play inside him.
That's how he put it, stay inside me and listen with your wrists.

When Mrs. McCabe came down to say they caught the man
who killed the president, he dropped the needle on "Opus One"
and said play. We listened to Krupa's "Rockin' Chair"
and Buddy Rich's big band doing "Time Check."

Lying on their sides, quarts of bourbon behind cans
of dried paint. You make the high-hat bark,
a sixteenth-note. You don't keep time, you make time.
The standards, renowned yet open to reinvention,
thus eternal. But I lived inside a body, Mrs. McCabe returned
from the hospital with no breasts, a week later
she was playing piano upstairs while Frank critiqued –

Don't play with your whole arm, it looks cool
but it isn't. He lit a Winston. Don't be like a bass player,
use deodorant. Never let a wimp carry your gear.
Listen carefully to the songs you hate the most.

Verse and chorus, shuffle, bridge, fill, drag, fill, stop-time,
ghost-note. Rumble of the sagging boiler, steam knocking the pipes.
Soon you won't have to remember, you'll just make the sound.

Dance

~ Bruce Smith

Is this it or am I waiting [with you] for the shiny cover to get torn off
by scuffing, by wind and incident? I had this dream I was kicking it,
can
in the street style. 45 minutes after I was born I could mime the
curious
contortions of mother's form, father's oceanic mask, then dusk with
old-world
sparrows and new world hungers to tear off the husk. I could mimic
this.
And clouds I could do – some fluffy, some mushroom, some fists.
45 minutes later I wanted to be Aeschylus and enter the beautiful body
of Prometheus as he thieved stuff and set it down before the dreaming,
infantile citizens, ingrates, who could now write and bake and
remember
but would forget the gift after wine and dinner theater. Like mother
and father they walk unhappy before me like gigantic forms morning
my missteps,
walk the other way with more Rorschachs of my overgrippng it,
overthinking it, then
stand still and scold my face as they'd sober. One generation's drunken
orders
are another's liver problems. I can't wait for the bad dream to be over as
they idle
in the power I, uh, relayed. Because I had the skill to smash and grab
the fire
and miscellaneous vowels, I did the seizing as I was seized. I stole the
electric
and the heat. You'd be cold now, unaroused from your sleep and dream
machines, the toss about of your [our] existence. Please shoot me now
in the right side below my ribs and have a surgeon dig the bullet out in
the light

I brought back, thank you, from a distance you try to echo if you can't
    know.
I have a stitch in my side, but I still can dance. I want to show you the
    thing I do:
blown back [by wind and incident], bent, shuffle, slide, spin, the
    repeated
rising up on the toes of my sneakers [my Nikes] and this move I stole
from Africa [jump, flex, freeze] and the electric current running through
    my body
I swear is not speeded up to confuse you [you're already confused]. I do
    this:
become puppet and I do this one backward but into the future. Tell me
    I'm not
in contact with another realm, some intoxicated goddess. Break back,
bruk up, bruk up, almost crippled, shot once and mime, snake charm,
whirl. Say what you will, I can mimic it before the bird comes down to
    snack.

Better Than Heaven

~ Charlie Smith

So many set asides, you say, intemperate
millionaires, those responsible for our welfare,
and individuals without malice
who goofed, the jail cells of our misery
damp with the morning chill, you say, done with, ruined,
the worst has happened, those we trusted, trimmers
at Zabar's carving the lox, and the wisdom
of children, finished, comparisons invalid,
the stupefied escape artists
and ministerial candidates and the self-satisfied
disposed of,
the rescued returned to the floods
and fruit pickers, those who catch beauty
aflight on the sweet-smelling breeze, authentic characters
messed up, dead on the floor
of western motels, crapped out jinxed, lost
to the boulevards, you say, past saving,
charlatans and poseurs, the wise, minxes in damaged fur coats,
drapers and stevedores
watching cartoons reflected in project windows, even
this compared to that, you say, and metaphorically, antique cars
gathering dust in apartment house garages,
old ladies getting sick from their cats, drunks,
homeless women fat on starch, the confused,
young boys ready to die, those still able to capitalize
and producers of change, you say, erased,
gone over, discontinuous, possibly lost,
ruffians and finicky brutalizers
and brilliant talkers, the fake, well-wishers
and party-boat captains, those out on bond, the repairmen
just now popping the lids on their coffees, you say,
sailors unmissed drowned, and wives

up for spousal abuse, unaccounted for
now, exhausted in little byways
out of the light, something, you say, better than heaven,
replacement crews undone, lovers hexed, something about this
tremendously appealing, you say, the quiet
in the abandoned mining camps,
the little trails across the desert that turn into artworks,
leads, possible meaning.

Forum Boarium
- Ron Smith

"...a civilized society is one exhibiting the five qualities of truth, beauty, adventure, art, peace." —Alfred North Whitehead

"North Korea Puts Nuclear Threats on Hold in Favor of Business, Skiing and Mushrooms." —*New York Times* headline

Romans roar through
on their way to the beach.
As always, Asians line up to get their hands bitten off
by a ancient manhole cover
they saw in a movie.
I'm on the hot seat (travertine), where
the sweet fountain water's cool from a Coke can.

Oleanders and parasols, sulfur and asphalt,
a wheezing bus, a Vespa chafing at the crosswalk . . .

The Temple of Hercules Victor explodes
with sunlight, Hercules Olivarius, choose your poison.
In the summer it hurts to look.
I'm guessing Mussolini
squashed that Coolie hat on it.
How can they stand the heat, stand the line, stand
so patiently with their little paper fans?
The one Caucasian couple quarrels and whines.

And the Mouth of Truth? Nothing but a shadow
behind its black bars.

Cut off from the river by the angry traffic: Hercules,
indeed, oldest marble building in Rome,
capitals luxurious with acanthus, a gift

of Lucius Mummius, who went at Corinth like
a sponge on a stick, wiped the isthmus
clean of its stinking Greeks.
Did he know Sparta had refused Corinthian
demands to raze Athens
three hundred years before?

I find no record
of a Mummius sense of justice. Or humor.

These twenty Corinthian capitals—and every man in Corinth
beheaded. To Mummius, it was, as we say, bidness.
He thought the loot could be replaced
if the ships went down.
That Philistine Mummius Hell-

enizing Rome . . . So much irony, so little time. Imagine
Japan, China, Korea, the whole
whopping East
one-handed at its keyboards in the fall!
Last summer on the Corso: a beggar with no hands at all . . .
Speak, O, Bocca della Verità! Tell us that

Caca lives yet! The sun's her hydrogen bomb!
Non licet omnibus adire Corinthum!

Blau Sein Hour

- Lisa Russ Spaar

The dark comprehendeth moi.
I mean, *not.* Does this mean,

Ladle of Light, any less or more
than the fiction you imbue

of gnosis? Unknow me,
if you do. Both of you.

Only so much can be
explained. Blue almond,

avenue by which we,
each of us, enters this world,

unless I'm missing something,
is rupture & suture.

Am I drunk? Always.
But not the way you think.

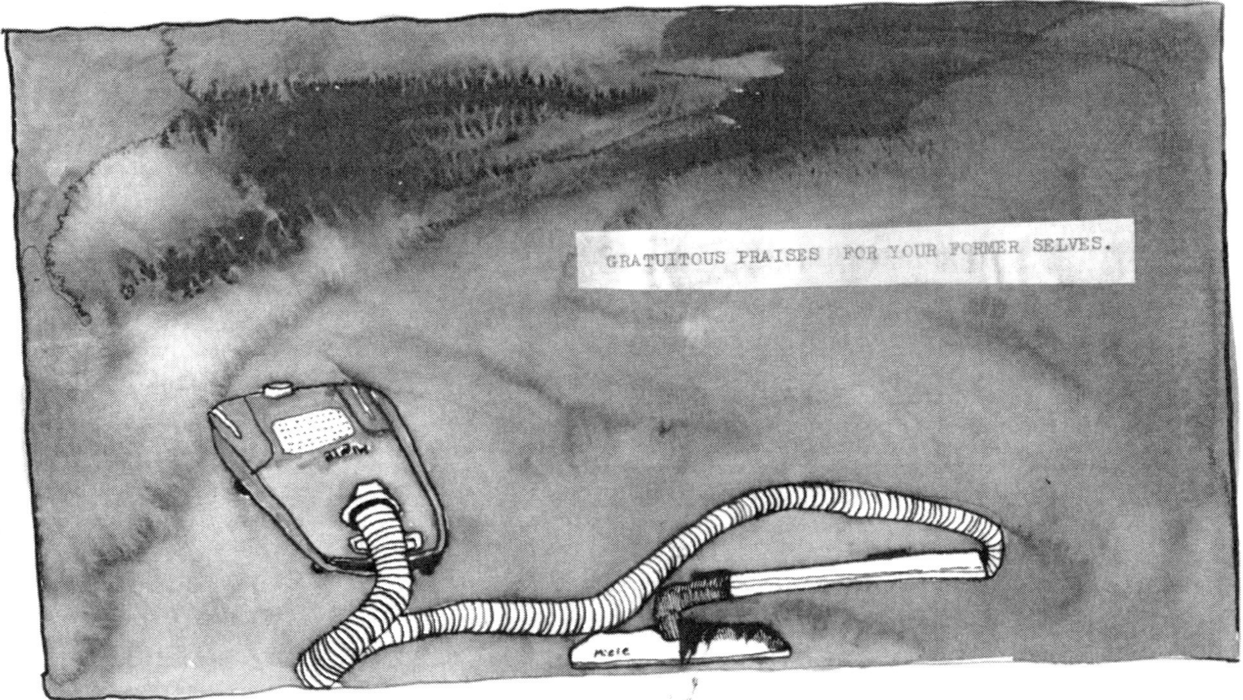

~ Bianca Stone

~ Bianca Stone

~ Bianca Stone

Riviera Terrors

- Terese Svoboda

Plug in a tree,
          even a palm, the bird—
make it black, not
                    raven but ravenous,
                              loud in the palm
upsidedown as in an Escher
          of village life,
                    (a few people walk the hills,
under bridges)
                    —and plants perpendicular at least,
                              a concession.

A blue car presses the nap
                                        of macadam
                              fresh dripped.
You've pressed that button,
                    and the bird's wings sticky,
                    why it's so hungry
                    and loud.

The blue car
                    out of a Hitchcock flick
          (scream that)
                              where color
          is fierce
(dream that)
and the back halves
of olive groves menace
                                        (see the game
your son plays)

      audio: the laundry
      audio: chair scrape

(don't forget the bird)

   ocean + ocean + ocean
   both up and down, the way
         gravity can surprise you—
the horizon.
      The plate of it, as blue
   as the streaming car
            full of fish as devious
   as *Notorious*,
         (the plate, not the car)
upends.

   You have to amass land
   to perturb,
         the anger and ardor kept under
oil and water
   that the bird has its beak full of
            below, the fish eating each other—

      (Picture that:
      dogfish eating dogfish.)

Glimmer Train

~ Arthur Sze

Redwinged blackbirds in the cattail pond—
today I kicked an elk hoof off the path,
read that armadillo eaters can catch
leprosy, but who eats armadillo and eats
it rare? Last night you wrote that, walking
to the stables, you glimpsed horses at twilight
in a field. We walk barefoot up a ridge
and roll down a dune; sip raki, savor
shish kebab and yogurt in an arcade.
Once we pored over divination lines incised
into tortoise shells, and once we stepped
through the keyhole entry into a garden
with pools of glimmering water. In the gaps
between my words, peonies rise through hoops
behind our bedroom—peonies are indeed
rising through hoops behind our bedroom—
you comb your hair at the sink as they unfold.

Reading Meister Eckhart at The Rock Bottom Bar

~ Daniel Tobin

> *The soul is far more closely united with God than are*
> *the body and soul… far closer than if one were to pour*
> *a drop of water into a cask of wine.*

From the farthest back booth Kelly calls
the bar to order—tonight, Trivial Pursuits,
with Kelly ("I'm Kelly," she reminds us),
while into the emptiness inside my glass
the bartender pours another IPA
freshly tapped as from a bottomless source
ever effluent in the depths, and lifts it,
lucent chalice, cup that substantiates the froth
of my want, onto the coaster's outsized host
here in the raw, thrum and rattle of time.
"Who was the first to reach the North Pole?"
Though on the page the Mesiter's question
posits the lure of a remoter axis:
Bullitio: the eternal boiling, primal efflux,
Godhead flowing out from Godhead into
Father, Son and Holy Spirit, a shared laugh
as the Meister tells it, of divine *jouissance.*
And where I am, as I raise my glass,
and Kelly prods with another query,
and the Keno player two seats over
scratches numbers in lead, staring at random
patterns on a screen, his dreamt riches,
appears to be a secondary flowering:
Ebullitio: this mediate stream, a current
out of eternal Confluence never-ending,

its melting forth in the shadow of nothing,
so the Meister would have it, for we are
thrown by being into multiplicity,
what we should shun, the nothing that is not,
the nothing that is, and everything virtual
as these televisions' bright, pixilated squares,
their alternate lives, the spirit rows
hierarchies doubled against a mirrored wall.
"What word makes its end its beginning?"
Kelly poses now from her niche of answers.
The mirrors here shimmer with patrons
at the rail, the greater in puzzled conclave,
and me at my book who never expected
to see Christ as a kind of palindrome,
the whole unfolding of this possible path
a flowing forward only to double back
to fare forward again, as the Meister says,
since the only purpose of God is birth—
the eternal birth of Christ in the soul,
though life in time is grief and restlessness,
and *where the creature stops there God begins to be,*
for as the Meister knew one can't see God
as one sees a cow, and as the Meister asks
as Kelly wouldn't, "Why does the Imageless
give form to life in images when everything
must free itself from this condition,
empty itself in form and name, as the Godhead
emptied itself from itself, in the image of Christ,
Godhead beyond God an unspoken word
that utters the Word that begets the world?"
Though I see how even the strictest mind
turns to *The Daily Race,* digital thoroughbreds
captive in the illusion of forward motion,
straining along the screen for each payoff,
while *esse simpliciter,* the negation of negations,

sustains within and beyond all longing
in its Eternal Now. But now, this now,
Kelly's moved on to the obscurities
of stardom, geography, top forties hits,
the plots and passions of TV sit-coms—
all the drift that attaches to the mind
or does not, or floats free, unhappily,
so you fail to win the thirty dollar gift
while that which the Meister claims you'll be
looks back on the self you have become
the way you might look at a worm in shit,
not because your life is dung and detritus
but because what it will become it is
at the core, so the Meister says, before God
was God, became God becoming, here,
where the fly and the soul lift in God's love
equally, where in hell what burns away
is nothing, the nothing your soul embraced:
trivia, like the instruments dangled bloody
in Avignon before the old man's eyes,
Heresy is of the will, not of the intellect,
the defense of the God-intoxicated man
who had glimpsed the stillness of God's first glance
in chaff and spindrift, extravagance and stain—
God seeking Godhead in a wilderness of names.

Mr. Fix-It

- William Trowbridge

Cursed by the broganed gods who govern tools,
my father turned Laocoön with power cords

and garden hoses, Blind Pew with drills
and hammers. Screws talked back, nails went

rubbery, saws turned piraña. He'd sweat,
fumble, curse his way through the gauntlet

of "Directions," jamming a half-inch bolt
in the hole for a quarter-inch dowel, joining Tab A

to Extension N, skipping the ambiguous
Step 5a. "God damn it," he'd declare

to the unresponsive skies; "lousy son of a bitch,"
he'd save for our electric mower, whose cord

he'd sever every other turn. A combat vet
with two Bronze Stars, he soldiered on

till the day he bought the canister of "Gro-Brite,"
advertised to turn your lawn "lush

as the greens at Pebble Beach." An I.E.D.
in his uncertain grip, it worked by pumping air

to force the liquid out the nozzle. He took
the contents in the face, the metal lid

grazing an ear. There was no talk at dinner,
only the A.C. chuckling under the window.

I Keep Scaring Myself

~ Chase Twichell

The distant fields lie fallow,
no longer even grazed.
Someday I'll be a plough blade
of pelvis, a few long bones.

I keep scaring myself,
but not about the body.
It's about the veils, which feel,
if I raise my arms, like wings—

feathers of white sky, word-tatters
in which I conceal myself,
asleep in the leaf-shadows,
lulled by the river of afternoons,

its squander of underwater lights.
I'm forgetting whole continents of cloud.
Part of me wants to go live
with the woman in a nursing home

whose suitor brings her the same
gold earrings every day in a box
with fresh paper and ribbons.
Each time I see them is the first time.

FROM WAVES AND LADDERS
~ translated by Alex Cigale

A stone's face is on the inside.

There, it is in motion. There, the red and black concatenations of jasper slide past one another. They shift their rough-worn surfaces of shell chalk. The rings of cave onyx flex and pulsate, contracting and expanding. A green light perambulates within the emerald's crystal.

When we split a stone, it manages to turn its face away in time and only the back of its head remains visible—solid and immovable. Thus a stone's death arrives—when the space for its movement becomes too confined. But its motion does not become extinct, so that sand is never still, it rushes the river and the wind. And it reverts to the interior, and again becomes stone, to whisper inaudibly, from behind the yellow-brown sliver.

A tree's strivings are all outward—from under the earth with its trunk, from under the bark with its leaves. A stone's soul is unlike such an open a book. It is concentrated and lonely. It knows not to expect help from the outside. It itself will become a wall and a stronghold. It is dependable.

A stone does not strive to make itself attractive with little bright shoots, sweet water, shade or shadows. It lies silently—on the surface or a mile beneath the surface—it would not presume to call to anyone randomly. It will look cautiously on those approaching and wait. It has time enough for everything.

It might perhaps allow you to remove its fragile shell. This will make its color and light visible. Colors, a metallic flash, a broken ray. They are cold and need no visitors—like the flower needs no bee. The stone continues to wait. It is testing—if this flicker is all that is required of it.

In the stone's center, to which its face is turned—a black point, the apex of a cone, uncoiled from the time the stone has come to glimpse. A stone speaks into it, and with it. The locus of all the stones' convergences is the locus of all our convergences with stone.

Из Волны и лестницы

~ original by Alexander Ulanov

Лицо камня внутри.

Там он движется. Проползают друг по другу черные и красные сгустки яшмы. Шевелят шершавыми ножками раковины мела. Пульсируют, сжимаясь и разжимаясь, кольца пещерного оникса. А внутри кристалла изумруда ходит зеленый луч.

Если камень расколоть, он успеет отвернуться, и виден будет только его затылок – твердый и неподвижный. Так приходит к камню смерть – когда пространства для движения становится слишком мало. Но движение не пропадает, и песок не стоит, он подгоняет реку и ветер. И он уйдет в глубину, и снова станет камнем, и будет неслышно шуршать за желто-коричневым сколом.

Дерево стремится наружу – из-под земли стволом, из-под коры листьями. Камень не так простодушен. Он сосредоточен и одинок. Он знает, что помощи ждать неоткуда. Он будет стеной и опорой сам. Он надежен.

Камень не стремится привлечь к себе яркими лепестками, сладкой водичкой, тенью. Он лежит молча – на поверхности или в километре от нее – и не станет звать кого попало. Он будет смотреть на подошедшего и ждать. Времени у него достаточно.

Может быть, он разрешит снять с себя корку. За ней будут цвет и свет. Краски, металлический блеск, преломленный луч. Они холодны и не нуждаются в пришедшем – как цветок в пчеле. Камень продолжает ждать. Он проверяет – только ли блеск нужен от него.

В центре камня, куда обращено его лицо, – черная точка, вершина конуса, развернутого в увиденное камнем время. Камень говорит в нее и ей. Точка встречи всех камней, точка встречи с камнем.

Self-Portrait, Rembrandt, 1660

~ Jean Valentine

I can't look up out of the sadness
only here along with your sadness

In the line of your black hat   the line
around the crown of my head gets stronger
when people come & go between us

From the first time I saw you
you held me in your understanding exhaustion.

An Occurrence at . . .

~ Arthur Vogelsang

Mercy and Miracles were guarantees
They came in needles
Softened your body's big ebony splinters
Softened the gray tin in your feet
And the number of Miracles
And the amounts of Mercy
Were not strained
They were a Quick Service
For enormous numbers who had gray tin
And ebony splinters in their bodies
The Quick Service Building also had a cafeteria
For enormous numbers of companions who did not need Mercy
One companion was with a suffocating friend
Suffocating takes a long time and can be stopped
The Building had restrooms (what a euphemism!)
For enormous numbers of relatives
Who did not personally need some Miracles
One relative was with a relative who was strangling
Strangling takes a long time and can be stopped
After three hours companions and relatives needed to pee
And to pretend to be hungry
To get away from their persistent groaner
Whose Mercy had not yet manifested
In Miracles which would possess him
In three long more hours
The Building was for emergencies
They gave you the needle
Immediately and you didn't pay six months later—
Part of the Mercy—
The Miracle was more in the needle
So it was a popular joint
The gig of choice for the desperate

So all the rooms were filled
And many more groaners lined the hallways
On highly professional slender beds
It was noisy
No flashes and booms signaling a Miracle
But clanking of thirty carts
And clanking of sixty voices
There was a religious rule
About not having water
Until the doctor said so
Doctors were the most important people there
Did not have to raise their voices
But their assistants yelled a
Number or one-word jokes
The groans of the groaners
Mostly groans for water
Added to the noise a lot
The joint didn't scrimp on lights
Somebody in unsupportable anguish from eye pain said, It's so bright in here.
The super bright light
Was to allow the proper insertion of needles
In the exact correct pore!
So understand please
The fluorescent brightness
Did not strain the quality of Mercy
Sometimes they had to use a knife
To get to the dark pink part
Where the needles went in
So they *planned* on lots of light
Companions and relatives
What about taking a break
To go to the cafeteria
With its ambient quiet shadows
And the ambience of quiet sunlight

Through the nine big windows
I promise nobody in the cafeteria
Will claim their brains are on fire
As I sat in the noisy hall on a folding chair beside her
As she lay in her highly professional slender bed kept against the wall
As I sat in the hall waiting for my beloved's Miracle
(Plenty of Mercy had already been stuck in)
While she lay nearly asleep
On a professional bed kept against the wall
Water roared in her ears
And a paper cup of water
Spilled on the hall floor
Looked like a creek she said
And how odd to see a creek
In any building but I see one she said
In our fantastically bright fantastically noisy hallway
As I sat there while she lay not dying
Her gray doom washing away
In the swift illusory creek on the floor
And in the creek-filled
Semi-permanent long needles in her
As I sat looking at the other dozen beloveds
On beds in the fluorescent hallway
A call came to a doctor
On his hand-held device
And a blue light went around in our hall's ceiling
Just when you thought
There could be no more light in the super fluoresence
Also a metallic whining sound occurred from
The twisting blue light beast
Down the hall from it
Two firemen and three cops wheeled toward us fast
A professional slender bed
With a mostly naked black guy
Quick into the nearest room

(I could touch the swiftly moving bed from where I sat
And touch the door of the room from where I sat)
They turned without whacking
Into my beloved's bed
Clearing it and me by about three inches
Into the room
Where the doctor had assembled five people
Of course I could hear pieces of their talk
That the black guy had been shot
Of course I saw his silver earrings
Of course everyone who was there
Had decided in the last century
That a black thug gutshot
Would be guaranteed
Mercy and Miracles, no exceptions,
Even if he could pay only in cash immediately
But still refused to pay
Six months later
The cops had rather huge square
Pistols on their hips
And the little woman cop also had
(What I later found out was)
A tear-gas pistol in her belt
Above her tummy
She and the cops stayed
In the gutshot guy's room
As if five other people with knives and a Mercy Mask
That held him to the bed
As if pushing him down into the bed
As if they and That
Couldn't keep him from fleeing
As he lay so still
I peeked into the room and compared the stillness
Of his body
To the stillness of my beloved's body

And there was no comparison
Sure, she didn't move for an hour more
When she got up and walked on water (the little spilled) to our car
But now he was like hardened year-old asphalt at 3 a.m. on a carless
street.

Bush

~ Diane Vreuls

Warms thieves.

.

For delay.

.

Feeds on balls, candy wrappers, leaves.
See: Hoover Bush

.

For confusions. Fists. Bursts. An argument at the knees.

.

Keeps bees.

.

DO NOT PRUNE

.

Not to be confused with short trees.

Should be wider than tall.
Its many tongues and shallow roots
produce particularly high-pitched songs.

.

Questions:

1. Can you eat the berries?
2. Why does it bud in winter?
3. Is it truly jolly or is it jealous?

.

Outlets:

Increasing. Once seen only in backrows
of nurseries, now available in dollar stores.
In groceries, next to pineapple. By mail.
Think of opening a used bush lot in Elyria.

.

Buy 1
Get 3 moles free.

.

As a memorial.

The Alice B. Gamboe Bush.
The Bush National Forest.

Hides weak legs, soil scars,
headstones. But cranky.

.

For protection against small losses.

A bush at Gila Bend
caught my uncle in a duststorm.
A Fairview Avenue bush
caught my report card.
Cowcatcher.
Stops babies rolling into the sea.
Plant a bush at each door and keep
your house at home.

.

NEVER PRUNE

.

Genesis of.

.

Religion of.

Burns when frightened.
Likes stutterers.

.

Loyalty of.

In 1956 a bush ambled from Moroni, Utah, to Still-
water Florida in pursuit of its owner who retired.
When interviewed in Missouri is reported to have said:
"People along the way have been wonderful, wonderful!"
It shames us. Have we lost the habit of travelling with
bushes? Your great grandmother took a rosebush west
in a wagon. But you've never taken your lilac for even
a Sunday drive.

.

The Nancy Drew Bush.

Her finger to her mouth, the old, kidnapped lady
in the wheelchair is whispering to the slim titian-haired
girl on the other side of the hedge.

See: As a rendezvous for undisclosed persons.
See: Bridal Bush in Wales.

.

NEVER TAKE A LOAN FROM A BUSH

.

Famous Bushes in History.

Plymouth Bush
Edgar Allan Bush
The Liberty Bush

.

The Bush in Opera.

.

In Literature.

There was a man and he wasn't very wise
and he jumped into a bramble bush and
scratched out both his eyes. In the next
verse he gets them back again.
But see: Boscophobia

Beauty and the Bush.

Someone thought she'd never seen a poem
as lovely as a bush, but we don't remember
her name.

.

False Tales.

They do not spread rumors and uprisings.
They do not trip trees.
They do not deceive migrations.
If you break a branch you will not turn
into a hunchback.

Such myths are unkind and have done
little to promote understanding
between the bush and others.

.

Here you go round the mulberry bush.
It's hard to tell when you're done.

.

Fifty Years Ago Today: The Outbreak of the Bush War

Within three weeks a cessation of most hostilities.
Old campaigners can still be seen along sidewalks.
The Begging Bush: A National Problem.

‘

Interview With Oldest Living Bush

Q: Are you tired?
A: Bushed.

.

DO NOT CALL SHRUB

.

Offers Asylum

To snow.
To deserters.
To small librarians.

.

Watcher.

.

Worries windows.

.

Outpost.

.

Even one is a conclusion.

.

Uproot it: there's
               praise from the grass
               blame from the wind.

On Being Obnoxious

~ David Wagoner

It's not enough to have
bad taste, though it does work
sometimes, but what would love
        to eat you by then already
        has its slobbering mouth
        full of some part of you
and yours you'd rather not lose
before it realizes
it's made an indigestible,
        vile, disgusting mistake
        in putting even your smallest
        portion in a position
to go down the hatch. When it changes
its mind, regurgitates
what's left of you, leaves you
        less willing and much less able
        to go on being obnoxious,
        you're done for. It's far more effective
to let yourself be known
from afar or at least no nearer
than a not-very-close encounter,
        that everything you consist of,
        or in philosophical terms
        are, is extremely unlikely
to please the nose, the mouth,
the teeth, the tongue, the throat,
or the raw digestive system
        of a decent predator,
        and the preferred, time-honored carrier
        of your identity
should be in projectible form,
a liquid or a vapor
or just your colorful nature.

Diamond Dog, Unleashed in the Airport
~ Diane Wakoski

My old arms, like bolts of cloth
unfold, let go in the rapid unroll of silk
from its cardboard cylinder, and the leash
pours out from my fist like water
from a faucet. He is loose. The Diamond Dog
running through the airport, ahead of me
and quickly lost in the soprano sax
of "These Foolish Things."
                                        Surrender.
I surrender. I'm so spent,
looking for my brother, David,
who bent over to kiss me once in a dream/ then
the spilled amaretto the/ shaking torso/ the
unmitigated oblation of/ melody so/ innocent
it could/ be diamonds/
                                crushed/ as in velvet/ she,
against, copy/ the old words,
say, "we failed," that love wasn't
enough. Diamond Dog jumps
back into my arms/ I am not
allowed
to carry him on board,
so I speak the one spell I know:

"disappear,"

and this is the way you get through the airline doors,
through the gates of the underworld,
bending like cloth falling
off its bolt.

Elegy for the Third Person

- G.C. Waldrep

The genius of a soft blue shirt
is the tiny theater it opens
in the play friendship is projecting
against the warm
spine of a sleeping dog.
In the first part, from a distance
the numbers all look
like sonnets. In the second,
the book is a process-
server on the back streets
of love's own Cincinnati,
some wind's new crampons driven
into the decimal's hive-like wall.
In the third part, trace
of a blind tithe's heat in the land's
sigh's permeable misdirection.
You put it on, and then
you take it off, the ebbing scars
barren planets attracted
less to the body than to the body's
secret density. There is no
such thing as a *lease*
on pain. The green light you see
could be your own, if you are
flying upside down,
reflected in the hovering water.

Eclipse

~ Rosanna Warren

When we went looking for that eclipse
of the moon in mid-Manhattan, we turned
dizzied by silhouettes
of towers, and thought the moon was swallowed
by hulking walls. And only when
we headed home, did she appear:
rusted, a trace of menstrual red, half-
erased in her own ghostly blood
like the scraps of poems tacked to the screen porch wall
of the summer cottage. After a winter of snow,
wind, and rain-lash, they delivered themselves
shyly: ink muted, letters
drained of sense, in phantom script
still Hölderlin whispered: god is near
and hard to grasp
but where danger rises,
grows what saves…

But what did we know of saving?

RAM
~ Mark Wunderlich

He stands stamping in the pasture,
angry that I've come, angry
that I didn't come sooner with my pail
of grain. A topnotch of wool shields his eyes,
snagged with bits of hay, bunched with burrs.
He shakes his head, flares nostrils under a Roman nose,
curls a lip to show me his single row
of teeth like keys of a harpsichord—long,
ivory-yellow, pegged in a black gum.
In snow, he'll stand all day
by the hay feeder, fleece parting at the spine,
grease saving him from the worst of it,
staring into the source of the weather.
In April the shearing team will come
and tip him on his rump, ridding him
of year's worth of wool. He'll submit
to the indignity,
his fleece peeled back in flocculent rolls.
Back on all fours, he'll trot off
to find his flock, sniff his harem's
bare behinds, account for his many lambs,
that nurse desperately, confused
by their mothers' altered forms.
They call and call, while he remains calm,
stepping among his kind
assessing the newly naked.
Once he knocked me down
with a blow to my hip, three hundred pounds
and a thick skull crashed against my pelvis.
Sprawled in the mud and dung
I pulled myself through straw
while he backed up for another run.

Before he could I hit him
with a broken rail, cracked it
across his nose. He barely noticed.
Now he regards me
with golden ovine eyes,
rich with a pastoral flame.

Even a punkster should excel at something
~ translated by Steve Bradbury

Is it Ok if I come in, for if we practiced together
We could find a way of coping with just about anything
If you appear too passive who can blame you?
But then you can't go blaming me for typing so slowly
If I'm not cut out to be a typist I can proofread at least

There are so many things we barely know the half of
But there are always ways of coping with everything
Even a punkster should excel at something
Driving a car repairing a roof changing a light bulb
DJing at a nightclub or being someone's punching bag if nothing else

We can love
Until we come to understand each other
We can waste to
Death

What difference does it make if you're dyslexic?
Who cares if you have trouble writing or making sense of things?
When people accuse us of not getting into something deeply
We should cook up ways of getting deeply into something
Just look at me I'm right inside you now if that's not
Getting into something deeply what is?

We can love
Until we come to understand each other
We can waste to
Death

And when we have our disagreements we should just buckle down
Pitch in and paint the whole apartment
There are still so many mornings you and I could rise
Like babies opening their eyes

即便是龐克也要有一技之長
~ original by Hsia Yü

我可以進去嗎我們一起練習
我們會找到辦法應付一切
若你看起來被動那也不能怪你
你也不能怪我若我打字太慢
沒能當上打字員我可以當校隊

對許多事我們其實一知半解
但是想辦法度日應付一切
即便是龐克也要有個一技之長
修理屋頂駕駛汽車換裝燈泡
夜店打碟至少當個拳擊沙包

我們可以相愛到
互相瞭解為止
我們可以
浪費到死

閱讀困難癥有什麼關係
寫字困難理解困難又怎樣
有人責備我們不夠深入的時候
我們就要想辦法一起給他深入
看看我這樣在你裏面如果這
不叫做深入還有什麼是深入

我們可以相愛到
互相瞭解為止
我們可以
浪費到死

意見不合時我們就要一起出現
一起動手把整個房子油漆一遍
我們還可以在很多清晨一起醒來
像嬰兒一樣睜開眼睛

Contributors' Biographies

Kim Addonizio's most recent books of poetry are *Lucifer at the Starlite* (W. W. Norton, 2009) and the just-reissued *Jimmy & Rita* (Stephen F. Austin State University Press, 2012). Among her awards and honors are fellowships from the National Endowment for the Arts and the Guggenheim Foundation, two Pushcart Prizes, and a Commonwealth Club Poetry Medal.

Meena Alexander is the author of numerous collections of poetry, literary memoirs, essays, and works of fiction and literary criticism. She is Distinguished Professor of English at the City University of New York. Her volume of poetry *Illiterate Heart* (TriQuarterly Books, 2002) won the PEN Open Book Award. Her most recent book of poetry is B*irthplace with Buried Stones* (TriQuarterly Books/ Northwestern University Press, 2013).

Dick Allen is the current Poet Laureate for the state of Connecticut and the author of seven books of poetry, including *Present Vanishing* (Sarabande Books, October, 2008; winner of Connecticut Book Award in Poetry, 2009) and *This Shadowy Place* (St. Augustine's Press, 2014) which was awarded the 2013 New Criterion Poetry Prize.

Nathalie Anderson's first book, *Following Fred Astaire*, won the 1998 Washington Prize from the *Word Works*; and her second, *Crawlers*, received the 2005 McGovern Prize from Ashland Poetry Press; her third, *Quiver*, was published in 2011 by Penstroke Press. Anderson's poems have appeared in such journals as the *New Yorker, Nimrod, North American Review, Paris Review, Prairie Schooner, Southern Poetry Review*, among others.

Nin Andrews is the author of several books including *The Secret Life of Manne-quins,* (Katywompus Press, 2012) and *Southern Comfort,* (CavanKerry Press, 2010). She is also the editor of a book of translations of the French poet Henri Michaux entitled *Someone Wants to Steal My Name.*

Rae Armantrout, generally associated with the Language Poets, has published ten books of poetry, including *Versed* (Wesleyan University Press) which won the 2010 Pulitzer Prize in Poetry and the National Book Critics Circle Award. Rae Armantrout's most recent book of poems is *Just Saying* (Wesleyan University Press, 2013).

Gennady Aygi (1934-2006) was a Chuvash poet, widely acknowledged as a seminal influence on post-war Russian avant-garde poetry for his synthesis of traditional folk lyric and the work of such European poets as Paul Celan and the French poets he translated into Chuvash, a Turkic language. His friendship with Boris Pasternak attracted the attention of Soviet authorities and he was expelled from the Gorky Institute of Literature in 1958 for "composing a book of oppositional poems undermining the basic methods of socialist realism" (not published until 1993). Having written in his native Chuvash, following Pasternak's suggestion, he began to write poetry in Russian in 1960. His poems in this volume, "The Field: In the Heat of Winter" and "A Dream: Manuscripts" are from his book *Fields in the City, Pages to France.*

Angela Ball is a frequently anthologized poet and translator. She is an author of many books including *The Museum of the Revolution* (Carnegie Mellon, 1999) and the *Night Clerk at the Hotel of Both Worlds* (University of Pittsburgh Press, 2007), which received both the Mississippi Institute of Arts and Letters Award in Poetry and the Donald Hall Prize from the Association of Writers and Writing Programs.

J.T. Barbarese's most recent book is *Sweet Spot* (Northwestern University Press, 2012). His poetry has appeared in the *Atlantic Monthly, Poetry,* the *New Yorker*, and the *Times Literary Supplement.* The executive editor of *StoryQuarterly*, his essay "Politics 2013" has been selected as one of the winners of the 2013 Hazlitt Essay Prize.

Brian Barker is the recipient of various awards and honors, including two Pushcart nominations, an Academy of American Poets prize, and the 2009 Campbell Corner Poetry Prize. His first collection of poetry, *The Animal Gospels* (Tupelo Press, 2006), won the Tupelo Press Editor's Prize. *The Black Ocean* (Southern Illinois University Press, 2011), his second collection,won the Crab Orchard Open Competition in 2011. Barker teaches at the University of Colorado, Denver, where he co-edits *Copper Nickel.*

Robin Behn is the author of six collections of poems, including *Horizon Note* (winner of the Brittingham Prize) and *The Yellow House* (Spuyten Duyvil, 2011). She teaches at the University of Alabama.

Sophie Cabot Black, whose work has appeared in numerous magazines, is the author of three collections of poetry: *The Misunderstanding of Nature* (Poetry Society of America's First Book Award), *The Descent* (2005 Connecticut Book Award), and *The Exchange* (Graywolf Press, 2013).

Yves Bonnefoy, widely translated and often acclaimed as France's greatest living poet, has published nine major collections of verse, several books of tales, and numerous studies of literature and art. He has also served as the chief editor of an important dictionary of world mythology, in two volumes. He succeeded Roland Barthes in the Chair of Comparative Poetics at the Collège de France, and is perennially cited as a leading candidate for the Nobel Prize for Literature.

Daniel Bosch's most recent book of poetry is *Crucible* (Handsel Books, 2002). Recent poems, translations, essays, and book reviews have appeared in *The Huffington Post, The Daily Beast, The Cortland Review, B O D Y, The Offending Adam,* and *Berfrois*, where he is Senior Editor.

Steve Bradbury received a PEN translation fund grant for *Salsa* (a forthcoming Zephyr Press publication), a collection of 46 poems by the Chinese poet Hsia Yü. He lives in Taipei.

Christopher Buckley is the author of *Varieties of Religious Experience* (Stephen F Austin State University Press, 2013) and the winner of the Capmbell Corner Poetry Contest in 2013. He is a contributing editor for *American Poetry Review*. "Before Long" is from the forrthcoming *Back Room at the Philosopher's Club* (due Spring 2014, Stephen F. Austin State University Press.

Gaius Valerius Catullus (ca. 84–54 BC) was a Latin poet of the late Roman Republic. His surviving works continue to be widely read and have proven to be influential in poetry and other forms of art.

Alex Cigale's poems have appeared in *Colorado, Green Mountains,* and the *Literary* reviews, and online in *Asymptote, Drunken Boat,* and *McSweeney's*. His other translations from the Russian can be found in *Cimarron Review, Literary Imagination, Modern Poetry in Translation, New England Review, PEN America*, and *Washington Square Review*. A substantial selection of his translations of Alexander Ulanov is in the *Manhattan Review 15.2*; a tribute to Gennady Aygi is on the *Beloit Poetry Journal* blog.

Patricia Clark has won the Pablo Neruda/ NIMROD award and the Gwendolyn Brooks Prize, and was co-winner of the Lucille Medwick Award of the Poetry Society of America. She has also co-edited an anthology of contemporary women writers called *Worlds in Our Words*. Her most recent publication is *Sunday Rising* (Michigan State University Press, 2013).

Andrei Codrescu is is a Romanian-born American poet, novelist, essayist, and screenwriter. He has been a commentator for National Public Radio's *All Things Considered* since 1983. His most recent publication is *So Recently Rent a World: New and Selected Poems, 1965-2012* (Coffee House Press).

Andrea Cohen's poems and stories have appeared in the *Atlantic, Poetry,* the *Threepenny Review, Glimmer Train,* the *Hudson Review* and elsewhere. Her most recent poetry collections are *Kentucky Derby* (Salmon Poetry, 2011) and *Long Division* (Salmon Poetry, 2009). Her fourth collection, *Furs Not Mine*, will be published by Four Way Books.

Billy Collins' most recent book is *Aimless Love: New and Selected Poems* (Random House, 2013). His poetry has appeared in anthologies, textbooks, and a variety of periodicals, including *Poetry, American Poetry Review, American Scholar, Harper's, Paris Review,* and the *New Yorker*. He was U.S. poet laureate 2001-2003.

Martha Collins is the author of the book-length poem *Blue Front* (Graywolf, 2006), which won an Anisfield-Wolf Award and was one of the New York Public Library's 25 Books to Remember from 2006. Her most recent collections of poems are *White Papers* (University of Pittsburgh Press, 2012) and *Day Unto Day* (Milkweed, 2014).She has also published four earlier collections of poems, and three collections of co-translations of Vietnamese poetry.

David Colmer is a prize-winning translator of Dutch literature. Seagull Books, who published his translation of *Self-Portrait of an Other* by Cees Noteboom in 2012, has just published a new collection of Nooteboom's poetry, *Light Everywhere*, which includes the poem "Evening." 2013 saw the publication of *Even Now* (Archipelago) Colmer's representative collection of the poetry of Hugo Claus.

Rebecca Cook's recent publication *I Will Not Give Over* (Aldrich Press, 2013) was a finalist for the Alice James Books' Beatrice Hawley Award for 2012. Her chapbook of poems, *The Terrible Baby*, is available from Dancing Girl Press, and her novel, *Click*, is forthcoming from Kitsune Books in 2013.

Nicole Cooley, the author most recently of two collections of poems, *Breach* (LSU Press 2010) and *Milk Dress* (Alice James Books 2010). She has received the Walt Whitman Award from the Academy of American Poets, and the Emily Dickinson Award from the Poetry

Society of America. She directs the MFA Program in Creative Writing and Literary Translation at Queens College-City University of New York where she is a professor of English.

Peter Cooley has published eight books of poetry, seven of them with Carnegie Mellon. His most recent volume is *Divine Margins* (Carnegie Mellon, 2009). His forthcoming book is *Night Bus to the Afterlife.*

Josh Cook's novel *Trike and Lola in Synthetic American* is being published by Melville House in the winter of 2014.

Brian Culhane's poems have appeared widely in such journals as *The New Republic, The Hudson Review*, and *The Paris Review*. In 2007, he was awarded the Poetry Foundation's Emily Dickinson First Book Prize; his winning manuscript, *The King's Question*, was published by Graywolf Press in 2008.

Jim Daniels' recent books include *Birth Marks* (BOA Editions Ltd., 2013), *Having a Little Talk with Capital P Poetry* (Carnegie Mellon University Press, 2011), *All of the Above* (Adastra Press, 2011), and *Trigger Man* (Michigan State University Press, 2011).

Alice Derry received an M.F.A. from Goddard College (now Warren Wilson College) in 1980 and was taught by poets William Matthews, Lisel Mueller and Louise Glück. She has published six books of poetry including *Strangers to Their Courage* (LSU Press, 2001) and her most recent book, *Tremolo* (Red Hen Press, 2012).

Carl Dennis, winner of the Pulitzer Prize for his book *Practical Gods*, is the author of eleven books of poetry, including, most recently, *Callings* (Penguin Books, 2010). His work appears in numerous anthologies, including *Best American Poetry* and *Pushcart Anthology*. His forthcoming book *Another Reason* (Penguin Books) will be released in 2014.

W. S. Di Piero, winner of the 2012 Ruth Lilly Poetry Prize, is the author of eleven books of poetry; the most recent is *Tombo* (McSweeney's, 2014). His poems have appeared frequently in *Poetry*, the *New Yorker*, and *Threepenny Review*, and he has written for *The New York Times Magazine*, *The New York Times Book Review*, *The New Republic*, and other periodicals. His autobiographical essays have appeared twice in *Best American Essays*.

Stephen Dobyns has published thirteen books of poems, twenty-one novels, two books of essays on poetry and a book of short stories *Eating Naked* (Holt/Metropolitan, 2000). His most recent work is *The Burn Palace* (Blue Rider Press, 2013). *Black Dog, Red Dog* was a winner in the National Poetry Series and *Cemetery Nights* received the Poetry Society of America's Melville Cane Award in 1987.

Patrick Donnelly's books are *The Charge* (Ausable Press, 2003, since 2009 part of Copper Canyon Press) and *Nocturnes of the Brothel of Ruin* (Four Way Books, 2012). Donnelly is director of the Poetry Seminar at The Frost Place, an associate editor of *Poetry International* and, with Stephen D. Miller, co-translator of the Japanese poems in *The Wind from Vulture Peak: The Bud-dhification of Japanese Waka in the Heian Period* (Cornell East Asia Series, 2013). PatrickDonnellyPoems.com

Norman Dubie, author of more than 24 books, has received numerous national grants and prizes, including the Bess Hokin Award of the Modern Poetry Association. His work, widely anthologized, has appeared in virtually every major journal of poetry over the last three decades. His most recent book is *The Volcano* (Copper Canyon Press, 2010). His collected poems, *The Mercy Seat*, won the PEN USA Prize for Best Book of Poetry.

Denise Duhamel is the recipient of numerous awards, including an NEA fellowship, and has been anthologized widely. She is professor of English at Florida International University and the author of numerous poetry collections, including *Queen for a Day: Selected and New Poems*

(University of Pittsburgh Press, 2001) and *Blowout* (University of Pittsburgh Press, 2013). Duhamel is guest editor for *The Best American Poetry 2013.*

Angie Estes is the author of five books, most recently *Enchantée* (Oberlin College Press, 2013). Her previous book, *Tryst* (Oberlin, 2009), was selected as one of two finalists for the 2010 Pulitzer Prize. Her awards include a Guggenheim Fellowship, an NEA Fellowship in Poetry, a Pushcart Prize, and the Alice Fay di Castagnola Prize from the Poetry Society of America.

Kathleen Flenniken is the 2012-2014 Washington State Poet Laureate. Her books are *Plume* (University of Washington Press, 2012), and *Famous* (University of Nebraska Press, 2006), winner of the Prairie Schooner Book Prize and named a Notable Book by the American Library Association.

Translator **Stuart Friebert**, for whose first book of German poems Krolow wrote the afterword, had the great privilege of knowing and working with Krolow on a number of occasions. Enjoying "a lifetime right to translate" Krolow, he has published two volumes of Selected Poems: *On Account Of: Selected Poems of Karl Krolow* (The Field Translation Series) and *What'll We Do With This Life?: Selected Poems by Karl Krolow, 1950-1990* (Fairleigh Dickinson University Press). A third volume, *Puppets in the Wind: Selected Poems of Karl Krolow,* will appear in 2014 from Bitter Oleander Press. The author of a dozen books of his own poems, and a number of stories, memoir pieces, essays, and anthologies, Friebert has published nine other volumes of translations from the Czech, Italian, Romanian, Lithuanian, and German.

Jeff Friedman's sixth collection of poetry, *Pretenders*, will be published by Carnegie Mellon University Press in 2014. His poems, mini stories, and translations have appeared in many literary magazines, including American Poetry Review, Poetry International, Prairie Schooner, and The New Republic.

Tess Gallagher is a poet, essayist, fiction writer and collaborator in film. Among her many publications are *Dear Ghosts*, (Graywolf Press, 2007), *The Man from Kinvara: Selected Short Stories* (Graywolf Press, 2009), and her most recent, *Midnight Lantern: New & Selected Poems* (Graywolf Press, 2012).

Brendan Galvin is the author of sixteen collections of poems, with his most recent book, *Whirl Is King: Poems from a Life List* (Louisiana State Univ Press, 2008). *Habitat: New and Selected Poems 1965-2005* was a finalist for the National Book Award, and he was short-listed for a Pulitzer Prize for Winter Oysters in 1983.

Beckian Fritz Goldberg's most recent publications are *Egypt From Space* (Oberlin College Press, 2013) and *Reliquary Fever: New and Selected Poems* (New Issues Poetry & Prose, 2010). Her work has appeared widely in anthologies and journals. She has received many awards including the Theodore Roethke Poetry Prize, the Annual Poetry Award, The Field Poetry Prize and a Pushcart Prize.

Dana Golin was born in Riga, Latvia. Her poems in Russian have appeared in *Novy Zhurnal* and are forthcoming in *Storony Sveta* and *Gvideon*. Her translations are in *EM: a Review of Text and Image, Ice Floe* (University of Alaska-Fairbanks), *Big Bridge* (a tribute to Andrei Voznesensky,) and *Modern Poetry in Translation*; her other translations of Vadim Mesyats are in *Big Bridge* and *Cortland Review*. Until recently, she was an Assistant Professor of Psychology at the American University of Central Asia.

Dana Goodyear is a staff writer at the *New Yorker* and the author of two collections of poetry, *Honey and Junk* and *The Oracle of Hollywood Boulevard*, both of which were published by W.W. Norton. Her nonfiction début, *Anything That Moves: Renegade Chefs, Fearless Eaters, and the Making of a New American Food Culture*, appeared in the fall of 2013.

Jorie Graham won the 1996 Pulitzer Prize in Poetry for *The Dream of the Unified Field: Selected Poems 1974-1994* and served as a Chancellor of The Academy of American Poets from 1997 to 2003. Her numerous collections of poetry, include *Sea Change* (Ecco, 2008) and *Place: New Poems* (Ecco; Original edition, 2012). Among her many honors are a John D. and Catherine T. MacArthur Fellowship and a Morton Dauwen Zabel Award from The American Academy and Institute of Arts and Letters.

Jessica Greenbaum is the author of the award-winning poetry collection *Inventing Difficulty* (Silverfish Review Press, 2000) chosen by *Library Journal* as one of the year 2000's five best, and *The Two Yvonnes* (Princeton University Press, 2012). Her poems and essays have appeared in the *New Yorker*, the *Nation, Poetry, Southwest Review*, and elsewhere. She is the poetry editor of *upstreet.*

Kelle Groom's most recent poetry collection is *Five Kingdoms* (Anhinga Press, 2010). Her memoir, *I Wore the Ocean in the Shape of a Girl* (Free Press, 2012) is a *Library Journal* Best Memoir for the year 2011. Her work has appeared in *Best American Poetry 2010*, the *New Yorker, Ploughshares*, and *Poetry*, among others. She is a contributing editor to *The Florida Review.*

Kimiko Hahn is the author of eight collections of poetry—most recently, *Toxic Flora* (W. W. Norton & Company, 2011). She teaches at Queens College, CUNY, in the MFA Program for Creative Writing and Literary Translation.

Jennifer Michael Hecht is the author multiple books ranging from history to poetry. Her debut volume of poetry, *The Next Ancient World* (Tupelo Press, 2001) won the Poetry Society of America's Norma Farber First Book Award. Her most recent book of poetry, in which "Smells Like Every Grief I Meet" appears, is *Who Said* (Copper Canyon Press, 2013).

Bob Hicok newest book is *Elegy Owed* (Copper Canyon Press, 2013). In 2001, *Animal Soul* was a finalist for the National Book Critic's Circle Award. His poems have appeared in the *Southern Review*, the *New Yorker, Poetry*, the *Paris Review*, and *American Poetry Review* as well as in eight volumes of the *Best American Poetry* and four times in the Pushcart Prize anthology.

David Huddle's seventh book of poetry is *Blacksnake at the Family Reunion* (Louisiana State University Press, 2012). His work has appeared in the *New Yorker, Esquire, Agni, Shenandoah*, and the *Best American Short Stories.* He teaches writing at the Bread Loaf School of English and the Rainier Writing Workshop.

Andrew Hudgins is the author of eight books of poetry—most recently: *A Clown at Midnight* (Mariner Books, 2013)—and a memoir *The Joker* (Simon & Schuster, 2013). The Never-Ending received high critical praise and was a finalist for the National Book Award. He is a recipient of Guggenheim and National Endowment for the Arts fellowships as well as the Harper Lee Award.

T.R. Hummer's tenth book of poems, *Ephemeron*, was published by Louisiana State University Press in November 2011 and his second book of essays, *Available Surfaces,* was published by University of Michigan Press's Poets on Poetry Series in 2012. His work has appeared in the *New Yorker*, the *Atlantic, Harper's, Paris Review*, and *Georgia Review*, among many other journals and magazines.

Mark Irwin's seventh collection, *Large White House Speaking*, was released by New Issues in 2013, and included the poem "Elephants." His poetry and essays have appeared in many periodicals including the *American Poetry Review*, the *Kenyon Review, Paris Review, Poetry*, the *Nation* and the *New Republic.* He is a past winner of The Nation/ Discovery and James Wright Poetry Awards.

Judy Jordan's poetry collection, *Carolina Ghost Woods* (Louisiana State University Press, 2000), received the Walt Whitman Award and won the National Book Critics Circle Award. She is also the author of *60 Cent Coffee And A Quarter To Dance: A Poem* (Louisiana State University Press, 2005).

Pierre Joris is a poet, translator, essayist & anthologist. Recent publications include *Meditations on the Stations of Mansur al-Hallaj* (poems) from Chax Press and *The University of California Book of North African Literature*, co-edited with Habib Tengour. Forthcoming are *Barzakh—Poems 2000-2012* (Black Widow Press) & *The Collected Later Poems of Paul Celan* (FSG).

Katia Kapovich has published seven books of poetry in Russian and two in English, the latest *Cossacks and Bandits* (Salt, 2008). Her poems have appeared in the *London Review of Books, Poetry*, the *New Republic, Harvard Review*, the *Independent, Jacket*, and many others. She is a co-editor of *Fulcrum*.

Marilyn Kallet is the author of sixteen books, including *Packing Light: New and Selected Poems* and her most recent collection of poems, *The Love That Moves Me* (Black Widow, 2013). She has translated Surrealist poets Paul Eluard and Benjamin Péret, and contemporary Parisian poet Chantal Bizzini. Kallet is Director of the Creative Writing Program at the University of Tennessee, where she is also Nancy Moore Goslee Professor of English.

Christopher Kennedy is the author of four books, including *Ennui Prophet* (BOA Editions, Ltd, 2011). His first, *Nietzsche's Horse*, was re-issued as an e-book by Dzanc Books in 2013. His work has appeared in many print and online journals and magazines, including *Ploughshares* and *McSweeney's*. He is an associate professor of English at Syracuse University where he directs the MFA Program in Creative Writing.

Richard Kenney's most recent book of poetry is *The One-Strand River: Poems 1994-2007* (Knopf, 2012). His work appears in many magazines and journals, including the *New Yorker*, the *Atlantic*, and the *American Scholar*.

John Kinsella is founding editor of the journal *Salt* in Australia and serves as international editor at the *Kenyon Review*. His most recent volumes of poetry are *Divine Comedy: Journeys through a Regional Geography* (W. W. Norton, 2010) and *Jam Tree Gully* (W.W. Norton, 2011). "'Did He who made the lamb make thee?'" first appeared in the *Manhattan Review*.

David Kirby's collection *The House on Boulevard St.: New and Selected Poems* was a finalist for the National Book Award in 2007. Kirby is the author of *Little Richard: The Birth of Rock 'n' Roll*, which the *Times Literary Supplement* of London called "a hymn of praise to the emancipatory power of nonsense." His most recent poetry collection is *A Wilderness of Monkeys*. See also DavidKirby.com

Len Krisak is an award-winning poet and translator. His awards include a Robert Frost Prize, a Robert Penn Warren Prize, a Richard Wilbur Award and a Der-Hovanessian Translation Award. His work includes a complete translation of the odes of Horace and, most recently, a translation of the poet Publius Vergilius Maro titled *Virgil's Eclogues* (University of Pennsylvania Press, 2012).

Karl Krolow (1915-1998) was one of the giants of German Letters of the last century. He made his mark early and often, with poems, translations, and criticism, later adding prose to his staggering output, which includes more than thirty volumes of poems, among them several Selected tomes. He was a critic, a judge of literary competitions, and a president of The German Academy of Language and Literature (1972-1975).

Lance Larsen's most recent books are *Backyard Alchemy* and *Genius Loci* (University of Tampa Press, 2013). His work has appeared in *New York Review of Books, Paris Review, Kenyon Review*, the *New Republic, Threepenny Review, Southern Review*, the *Times Literary Supplement*, and elsewhere.

Sydney Lea's most recent books are *Young of the Year* and *I Was Thinking Of Beauty* (Four Way Books 2013). His stories, poems, essays and criticism have appeared in many periodicals including the *New Yorker*, the *Atlantic*, the *New Republic*, the *New York Times*, and *Sports Illustrated* as well as in more than forty anthologies. He is the Poet Laureate of Vermont.

Lyn Lifshin has published over 130 books and has edited three anthologies of women's writing including *Tangled Vines*, now in print for over twenty years. She is the subject of the documentary film *Not Made of Glass*. Her most recent publication is *A Girl Goes into the Woods* (NYQ Books, 2013).

William Logan's most recent book of poetry is *Madame X* (Penguin Books, 2012). He has published ten books of poetry and five of essays and reviews. He teaches at the University of Florida and lives in Gainesville, Florida, and Cambridge, England.

James Longenbach's recent publications are *The Iron Key* (W. W. Norton & Company, 2012) and a book of essays: *The Virtues of Poetry* (Graywolf Press, 2013). He is the Joseph Henry Gilmore Professor of English at the University of Rochester and has taught at the University since 1985. His poems have appeared in many periodicals including the *New Yorker*, the *New Republic*, the *Nation*, and the *Yale Review*.

Mary Mackey is the author of thirteen novels and six collections of poetry, including *Sugar Zone,* winner of the 2012 PEN Oakland Josephine Miles Award. Her poems have been praised by Wendell Berry, Jane Hirshfield, Dennis Nurkse, Ron Hansen, Dennis Schmitz, and

Marge Piercy for their beauty, precision, originality, and extraordinary range. In Spring 2014, Marsh Hawk Press will publish a new collection of her poetry entitled *Travelers With No Ticket Home.*

Maurice Manning's book, *The Common Man*, was one of the two finalists for the 2011 Pulitzer Prize in Poetry. His first collection of poems, *Lawrence Booth's Book of Visions* was awarded the Yale Younger Poets Award. His most recent book is *The Gone and the Going Away* (Houghton Mifflin Harcourt, 2013).

Campbell McGrath is the author of ten books of poetry, including *Spring Comes to Chicago, Florida Poems, Seven Notebooks*, and most recently *In the Kingdom of the Sea Monkeys* (Ecco Press, 2012) He has received many of America's major literary prizes, including Guggenheim Fellowship, a MacArthur "genius" Fellowship, and a Witter-Bynner Fellowship from the Library of Congress.

Sandra McPherson is the author of many books of poetry, including *A Visit to Civilization* (Wesleyan,2002) and her most recent, *Expectation Days* (University of Illinois Press, 2007). Her poems have appeared in many periodicals including the *New Yorker*, the *Paris Review, Poetry*, the *Southern Review*, and *TriQuarterly.*

Vadim Mesyats studied physics at Tomsk State University. In 1993 he emigrated to the USA, and worked for Stevens College in New Jersey as a coordinator of the Russian/American cultural program. The original of the poem appearing here was first published in *Novii Mir. Guest in the Homeland* (Talisman House, 1997) is his early Selected in English. He was short-listed for the Russian Booker Prize in 2002, for his novel *Treatment by Electricity*, and is the publisher of Russian Gulliver press.

Carol Moldaw's most recent book is *So Late, So Soon: New and Selected Poems* (Etruscan Press, 2010). She is the author of four other books of poetry, including *The Lightning Field*, which won the 2002 FIELD

Poetry Prize, as well as a novel, *The Widening*. Through the Window has been translated into Turkish, Chinese and Portugese and is published widely in anthologies and journals.

Cees Nooteboom is an essayist, poet and novelist and one of Holland's most renowned authors; awarded the Pegasus Prize, the Constantijn Huygens Prize, the Aristeon European Literary Prize, and frequently mentioned as a candidate for the Nobel Prize. The poem "Evening" is drawn from *Light Everywhere* (Seagull Books, 2014), a new collection of his poetry.

Idra Novey is the author of *Exit, Civilian* and *The Next Country*. Her recent translations include Viscount Lascano Tegui's novel *On Elegance While Sleeping*—shortlisted for the 2010 Best Translated Book Award—and Clarice Lispector's novel, *The Passion According to G.H.* (New Directions, 2012).

Sharon Olds is the author of eleven books of poetry. *The Dead and the Living* received the National Book Critics Circle Award, *The Unswept Room* was a finalist for the National Book Award and The National Book Critics Circle Award, and *One Secret Thing* was a finalist for the Forward Prize. Her most recent book is *Stag's Leap* (Knopf, 2012). She teaches at New York University.

Dzvinia Orlowsky is a poet and translator. She is the author of five collections of poetry published by Carnegie Mellon University Press including *A Handful of Bees*, reprinted in 2009 as a Carnegie Mellon Classic Contemporary, *Convertible Night, Flurry of Stones*, co-winner of the 2010 Sheila Motton Book Award and her most recent, *Silvertone*. A Pushcart Prize recipient and Founding Editor of Four Way Books, she is teaches in at the Solstice Low-Residency MFA in Creative Writing Program of Pine Manor College and at Providence College.

Ruth Padel is an award-winning British poet. Her nine collections include *Darwin—A Life in Poems* (Knopf 2009) and *On Migration:*

Dangerous Journeys and the Living World (Counterpoint 2013). She is Fellow of the Royal Society of Literature and Teaching Fellow in Poetry at Kings College London.

Michael Palmer is a poet and translator. In 2006, he received the Wallace Stevens Award from the Academy of American Poets. For over thirty years he has worked extensively with contemporary dance and has collaborated with many composers and visual artists. His most recent book of poetry is *Thread* (New Directions, 2011).

Linda Pastan is former Poet Laureate of Maryland. She has twice been a finalist for the National Book Award, and in 2003 she won the Ruth Lilly Prize for lifetime achievement. Her 13th book, *Traveling Light,* was published in 2011 by W.W. Norton & Company.

Carl Phillips is the author of many books of poems, including *The Rest of Love* and *Double Shadow*—both National Book Award Finalists. *Silverchest*—his most recent book of poems—was published by Farrar, Straus and Giroux. He teaches at Washington University in St. Louis.

Anzhelina Polonskaya was born in Malakhovka, a small town near Moscow. Her work has been translated into Dutch, Slovenian, Latvian, Spanish and other languages and has appeared in *World Literature Today, Poetry Review, American Poetry Review*, and *International Poetry Review*. In 2012 a bilingual edition of new poems was published by Zephyr Press under the title *Paul Klee's Boat.*

Kevin Prufer is the author of, among others, *In a Beautiful Country* and *National Anthem*. He has received three Pushcart Prizes, and awards from the Poetry Society of America, the Academy of American Poets, and The Lannan Foundation. His first book, *Strange Wood,* received the 1997 Lena-Miles Wever Todd Poetry Prize. Prufer's book *The Finger Bone* was reissued by Carnegie Mellon in 2013.

Christina Pugh's third book of poems, *Grains of the Voice*, is forthcoming in 2013 from Northwestern University Press. She is also the author of *Restoration* (Northwestern University Press, 2008) and *Rotary* (Word Press, 2004), which received the Word Press First Book Prize. Her poems have appeared in the *Atlantic, Poetry,* the *Kenyon Review, Ploughshares,* and other publications, and have been anthologized in *Poetry 180* and other anthologies. Her honors have included the Lucille Medwick Memorial Award from the Poetry Society of America, an individual artist fellowship in poetry from the Illinois Arts Council, the Grolier Poetry Prize, and residencies at the Ragdale and Ucross Foundations. She is an associate professor in the Program for Writers at the University of Illinois at Chicago.

Lia Purpura's books include *On Looking: Essays, King Baby* (winner of the Beatrice Hawley Award) and *Rough Likeness: Essays* (Sarabande Books, 2011). Her awards include NEA and Fulbright Fellowships, three Pushcart prizes, *Best American Essays 2011*, the AWP Award in Nonfiction, and the Ohio State University Press Award in Poetry.

Lawrence Raab's collection of poems, *What We Don't Know About Each Other*, won the National Poetry Series and was a Finalist for the 1993 National Book Award. Among his books are T*he Probable World, Visible Signs: New & Selected Poems, The History of Forgetting* and *A Cup of Water Turns into a Rose* (Adastra Press, 2012).

James Richardson's most recent books are *By the Numbers: Poems and Aphorisms*, which was a finalist for the National Book Award, *Interglacial: New and Selected Poems and Aphorisms,* a finalist for the National Book Critics Circle Award, and *Vectors: Aphorisms and Ten-Second Essays*. Winner of the 2011 Jackson Poetry Prize, he teaches at Princeton University.

Alberto Rios is the author of several collections of poetry, including *Dangerous Shirt* (Copper Canyon Press, 2009); *The Smallest Muscle in the Human Body*, which was nominated for the National Book Award;

and *Whispering to Fool the Wind*, which won the 1981 Walt Whitman Award.

David Rivard's most recent book is *Otherwise Elsewhere: Poems* (Graywolf Press, 2010). *Wise Poison* won the James Laughlin Prize from the Academy of American Poets. His poems and essays appear in the *American Poetry Review, TriQuarterly, Ploughshares, Poetry London*, and many other magazines. In 2006, Rivard was awarded the Hardison Poetry Prize from the Folger Shakespeare Library.

Hoyt Rogers divides his time between the Dominican Republic and Italy. His poems, stories, essays and translations from the French, German, Italian, and Spanish, have appeared in a wide variety of periodicals. He has published over a dozen books of poetry, criticism, editions and translations. His most recent translation is *Second Simplicity*, a collection of verse and prose by Yves Bonnefoy.

J. Allyn Rosser's first collection of poems, *Bright Moves*, won the Samuel French Morse Poetry Prize. She is the recipient of many awards including a Pushcart Prize and fellowships from the National Endowment for the Arts. Her fourth collection of poems, *Mimi's Trapeze*, is forthcoming from University of Pittsburgh Press. She teaches at Ohio University and serves as editor-in-chief of the New Ohio Review.

Clare Rossini is the author of three collections of poetry: *Lingo; Winter Morning with Crow;* and *Selections from the Claudia Poems.* Her poems and essays have appeared in a range of journals and anthologies, including *Poetry*, the *Paris Review, Ploughshares*, the *Kenyon Review, Poets for a New Century*, and the *Best American Poetry*.

Tomaž Šalamun lives in Ljubljana, Slovenia. He taught Spring semester 2011 at Michener Center for Writers at The University of Texas. His recent books translated into English are *Woods and Chalices, Poker, There's the Hand and There's the Arid Chair, The Blue Tower* and *On the Tracks of Wild Game.*

Mary Jo Salter's most recent book is *Open Shutters* (Knopf, 2013). An editor at the *Atlantic* and Poetry Editor of the *New Republic,* she is also a coeditor of the *Norton Anthology of Poetry*. Her poems have appeared in various anthologies and her essays and book reviews have appeared in the *New York Times Book Review,* the *New Republic*, the *Yale Review*, the *Atlantic*, and elsewhere.

Grace Schulman's newest book is *Without a Claim* (Mariner Book, 2013). Included in her acclaimed publications is *Days of Wonder*—a Library Journal Best Book of the Year. Her awards includea Guggenheim Foundation Fellowship and a Poetry Fellowship from the New York Foundation of the Arts. She was the Poetry Editor of the *Nation*, and former director of the Poetry Center, 92nd Street Y.

Maureen Seaton is the recipient of the NEA, Iowa Poetry Prize, the Lambda Literary Award for poetry, and two Pushcarts. Her memoir, *Sex Talks to Girls* (University of Wisconsin Press, 2008), also won a Lammy. Her recent poetry collection, *Fibonacci Batman: New and Selected Poems 1991-2011*, was published by Carnegie Mellon University Press in 2013.

Martha Serpas is the author of two collections of poetry, *Côte Blanche* (New Issues, 2002) and *The Dirty Side of the Storm* (W.W. Norton, 2009). Her work has appeared in the *New Yorker*, the *Nation, Southwest Review,* and *Image: A Journal of the Arts and Religion*, as well as in a number of anthologies, including the Library of America's American Religious Poems.

Alan Shapiro is the author of many collections including *Happy Hour*, winner of the 1987 William Carlos Williams Award and finalist for the National Book Critics Circle Award; *Mixed Company*, winner of the Los Angeles Times Book Award in poetry; and *Old War*, which won the 2009 Ambassador Book Award in poetry. His latest book is *Night of the Republic*, (Houghton Mifflin/Harcourt, 2012).

Laurie Simmons is a graduate from the Tyler School of Art in Philadelphia and is currently represented by Salon 94 in New York where she lives and works. Ms. Simmons has worked in set-up photography since the late 1970s and is best known for images involving female dolls that range from tiny plastic toy figures to human-size Japanese love dolls. Her most recent book is *The Love Doll* (Salon 94/Tomio Koyama Gallery, 2012). Recently the Aurora Picture Show presented Ms. Simmons with the 12th Annual Aurora Award.

Jeff Skinner has published numerous collections of poetry including *Late Stars, A Guide to Forgetting* (a winner in the 1987 National Poetry series) and the recently published *Glaciology*. His work has been included in many anthologies and have appeared in various periodicals such as the *New Yorker*, the *Atlantic*, the *Nation*, the *American Poetry Review* and *Poetry*.

Ron Slate's first book of poems, *The Incentive of the Maggot*, was published by Houghton Mifflin in 2005, nominated for the National Book Critics Circle poetry prize and was awarded the Bakeless Poetry Prize and the Larry Levis Reading Prize of Virginia Commonwealth University. *The Great Wave*—his second book—was published by Houghton Mifflin in 2009.

Bruce Smith is the author of six books of poems including *The Other Lover*, which was a finalist for both the National Book Award and the Pulitzer Prize, and most recently *Devotions*, a finalist for the National Book Award, the National Book Critics Circle Award, and the LA Times Book Prize. He received the 2012 William Carlos Williams Award.

Charlie Smith's most recent poetry collection is *Word Comix* (W. W. Norton & Co., 2009); others include *Women of America* (2004); *Heroin and other poems* (2000); *Before and After* (1995); and *The Palms* (1993). He has also published six novels, the latest of which is *Men In Miami Hotels*, (Harper Perennial, 2013). His newest book, *Jump Soul: New and Selected Poems*, will be out in March from W. W. Norton.

Ron Smith's latest book of poems is *Its Ghostly Workshop* (Louisiana State University Press, 2013). Smith is the winner of the Carole Weinstein Poetry Prize, the Guy Owen Award from *Southern Poetry Review*, and the Theodore Roethke Prize from *Poetry Northwest*. He has published poems and critical prose in many periodicals and anthologies.

Lisa Russ Spaar is the author and editor of eight collections of poetry, most recently *Vanitas, Rough: Poems* (Persea, 2012) and T*he Hide-and-Seek Muse: Annotations of Contemporary Poetry* (Drunken Boat, 2013). Her awards include a Guggenheim Fellowship, a Rona Jaffe Award, the Carole Weinstein Poetry Prize, and the Library of Virginia Award for Poetry. Her essays, reviews, and commentaries about poetry have appeared in the *Chronicle of Higher Education*, the *Washington Post*, the *New York Times*, the *Los Angeles Review of Books*, and elsewhere. She is a Professor of English and Creative Writing at the University of Virginia.

Alison Stine is the author of *Wait*, winner of the Brittingham Prize (University of Wisconsin Press, 2011); *Ohio Violence*, winner of the Vassar Miller (University of North Texas Press, 2009); and *Lot of My Sister*, winner of the Wick Prize (Kent State University Press, 2001). She teaches at Ohio University, where she is a Postdoctoral Fellow.

Bianca Stone is the author of several poetry chapbooks, including *I Saw The Devil With His Needlework* (Argos Books, 2012) and the illustrator of *Antigonick*. Her recent publication is *Someone Else's Wedding Vows* (Tin House Books, 2014). Her poems have appeared in many journals including *Best American Poetry 2011, Conduit, Tin House*, and *Crazyhorse*. PetryComics.com

Arthur Sze's most recent collection of poetry is *The Gingko Light*. His many awards include an American Book Award, a Lannan Literary Award and the Western States Book Award for Translation. He is a Chancellor of the Academy of American Poets.

Terese Svoboda's books include *Tin God* (University of Nebraska Press, 2013), *Pirate Talk or Mermalade, Bohemian Girl, Weapons Grade, Laughing Africa*, and *Trailer Girl.* Her work has appeared in the *Atlantic*, the *New York Times Literary Supplement*, the *Nation, Spin, American Poetry Review, Paris Review*, and the *New Yorker.*

Mary Szybist is the author of *Granted*, a finalist for the National Book Critic's Award in Poetry. Her second and most recent collection, *Incarnadine*, was published in 2013 by Graywolf Press. Her work appears in *Poetry, Kenyon Review, Iowa Review, Tin House*, and many other journals and reviews.

Michael Thomas Taren is a graduate of the Iowa Writer's Workshop. His chapbook, *08 September 2009*, was published by Factory Hollow Press, Amherst, MA. His translations of Tomaž Šalamun have been widely published. His book *Motherhood* was 2010 finalist for the *Fence* Poetry Series.

John Taylor is the author of the three-volume *Paths to Contemporary French Literature* and *Into the Heart of European Poetry*—all four books published by Transaction. He has also written many books of stories, short prose, and poetry, the latest of which are *If Night is Falling* and *Now the Summer Came to Pass.* He has translated books by Pierre-Albert Jourdan, Philippe Jaccottet, and Jacques Dupin and is currently translating Louis Calaferte's «Le Sang violet de l'améthyste.»

Daniel Tobin is the author of many books of poems and critical studies. His most recent publications are *The Net, Belated Heavens*, and *Awake in America.* His awards include the The Robert Penn Warren Award, a Robert Frost Fellowship, and creative writing fellowships from the National Endowment for the Arts and the John Simon Guggenheim Foundation.

William Trowbridge's new book, *Put This On, Please: New And Selected Poems* will be out from Red Hen Press in March. His poems have appeared in more than 30 anthologies and textbooks, as well as in various periodicals. His awards include an Academy of American Poets Prize, a Pushcart Prize, and a Bread Loaf Writers' Conference scholarship. He is the current Poet Laureate of Missouri.

Chase Twichell won the Kingsley Tufts Poetry Award in 2011. Her seventh and most recent book, *Horses Where the Answers Should Have Been*, was published by Copper Canyon Press in 2010. Her previous collections include *Dog Language* (2005) and *The Snow Watcher* (1998). A student in the Mountains and Rivers Order at Zen Mountain Monastery, she and her husband, the novelist Russell Banks, split their time between upstate NY and Miami.

Alexander Ulanov (1963) lives in Samara and works at Samara State Aerospace University. His books of poetry are *Wind Direction* (1990), *Dry Light* (1993), *Waves and Ladders* (1997), Displacements + (2007), *Methods of Seeing* (2012), and the book of prose *Between We* (2006). He has written more than 350 articles and book reviews about contemporary literature and received the Andrey Bely prize for his criticism (2009), having been short-listed in the prose category in 2007. In 2007, he was a Visiting Poet as a CEC ArtsLink Fellow at the International Writing Program at Iowa. Ulanov is himself a translator (of contemporary American poets, Dylan Thomas, Paul Valery, and of Rilke's "Sonnets to Orpheus").

Jean Valentine won the Yale Younger Poets Award for her first book, *Dream Barker*, in 1965. Her eleventh book of poetry is *Break the Glass*, (Copper Canyon Press, 2010). *Door in the Mountain: New and Collected Poems 1965–2003* was the winner of the 2004 National Book Award for Poetry. The recipient of the 2009 Wallace Stevens Award from the Academy of American Poets, Ms. Valentine has taught at Sarah Lawrence, New York University, and Columbia.

Arthur Vogelsang was an editor/publisher of the *American Poetry Review* from 1973-2006. *Twentieth Century Women* (University of Georgia

Press, 1988), was selected by John Ashbery for the Contemporary Poetry Series and *Cities and Towns* (University of Massachusetts Press, 1996) received the Juniper Prize. His most recent book is *Expedition: New & Selected Poems* (Ashland Poetry Press, 2011).

Diane Vreuls has published a novel, a collection of short stories, a children's book, and a book of poems, as well as work in the *New Yorker, Commonweal, Shenandoah*, and other magazines.

Andrew Wachtel is Professor of the Humanities at Northwestern University and a member of the American Academy of Arts and Sciences. He is the author of ten books and more than 100 articles on Russian and South Slavic literature, culture, and society. In 2004 he published *Anzhelina Polonskaya, A Voice: Selected Poems*. Polonskaya and Wachtel released a bilingual edition of Polonskaya's poems entitled *Paul Klee's Boat* (Zephyr Press, 2012).

David Wagoner has published 19 books of poems, most recently *After the Point of No Return*, (Copper Canyon Press, 2012). He has also published ten novels, one of which, *The Escape Artist*, was made into a movie by Francis Ford Coppola. He won the Lilly Prize in 1991, six yearly prizes from *Poetry*, two yearly prizes from *Prairie Schooner*, and the Arthur Rense Prize for Poetry from the American Academy of Arts and Letters in 2011. He was a chancellor of the Academy of American Poets for 23 years.

Diane Wakoski's newest collection of poems is *Bay of Angels* (Anhinga Press, 2013). She has published more than forty collections of poems, including *Emerald Ice: Selected Poems 1962-1987* (1988), which won the Poetry Society of America's William Carlos Williams Award.

G.C. Waldrep's most recent collection is *Your Father on the Train of Ghosts*, in collaboration with John Gallaher. Previous collections include *Archicembalo, Disclamor*, and *Goldbeater's Skin*. He lives in Lewisburg, Pennsylvania, where he teaches at Bucknell University and serves as Editor-at-Large for the *Kenyon Review*.

Rosanna Warren, the author of four collections of poetry, has received awards from the Academy of Arts and Letters and has won the Lamont Poetry Prize. Her most recent publication is *Ghost in a Red Hat: Poems* (W. W. Norton & Company, 2011). She teaches at the University of Chicago. "Eclipse" was commissioned by the Reva Logan Poetry Series at the University of Chicago.

Mark Wunderlich is the author of *The Anchorage*, which received the Lambda Literary Award, *Voluntary Servitude,* and *The Earth Avails* (Graywolf, 2014). His work has appeared in many periodicals and has been widely anthologized. He teaches literature at Bennington College in Vermont where he is also a member of the faculty of the Writing Seminars.

Hsia Yü is the author and designer of six volumes of groundbreaking verse and co-editor of the Taipei-based avant-garde journal *Xianzai Shi* (*"Poetry Now"*). A translation of her fourth collection, *Salsa,* is forthcoming from Zephyr Press.

April 10, 2015

Basquiat as a critic describes cancels to reveal.

AGO

Toronto

Yang Piano

CPSIA information can be obtained at www.ICGtesting.com
Printed in the USA
LVOW08s1832170315

430918LV00001B/50/P

9 781941 196021